THE TURN TO THE NATIVE

T0335195

The Turn to the Native

Studies in Criticism and Culture

ARNOLD KRUPAT

UNIVERSITY OF NEBRASKA PRESS: Lincoln and London

Acknowledgments for previously published materials appear on page xii.

© 1996 by the University of Nebraska Press
All rights reserved
Manufactured in the United States of America

♾ The paper in this book meets the minimum requirements of American National Standard for Information Sciences—Permanence of Paper for Printed Library Materials, ANSI Z39.48-1984.

First paperback printing: 1998

Library of Congress Cataloging-in-Publication Data

Krupat, Arnold.
The turn to the native : studies in criticism and culture / Arnold Krupat.
p. cm.
Includes bibliographical references and index.
ISBN: 978-0-8032-7786-1
1. American literature—Indian authors—History and criticism—Theory, etc. 2. Vizenor, Gerald Robert, 1934-   —Criticism and interpretation. 3. American literature—Indian authors—History and criticism. 4. Indians of North America—Civilization—Historiography. 5. Indians in literature. I. Title.
PS153.I53K77   1996
810.9'897—dc20   96-15152
                                                                                        CIP

For my mother, Ruth, my brother, Edward,
and in memory of my father, Milton Krupat

Contents

Preface

Each of the five chapters of this book in one way or another engages questions of identity as they shape the criticism of contemporary Native American literature. This is so in spite of the fact that, as I try to explain below, I am very wary of identitarian emphases in cultural criticism as in politics.

But for all my wariness, it is impossible to ignore the fact that we live today in a world in which boundaries and parameters are shifting to a degree unparalleled since the end of World War II. Western Europe lumbers toward "unification" while its great nation-states internally fragment along racial and religious lines. The Eastern European states, by some accounts newly "free," do not so much appear to have joined the heady world of the "post-"—postcolonial, postmodern, posthistorical—as, instead, to have begun to constitute a sorry series of "formers": the former Yugoslavia, the former Czechoslovakia, the former Soviet Union, and so on.

Here in the United States—I write in the fall of 1995—the "culture wars" that were so "hot" only a short time ago have settled into naked class warfare. Recent headlines announce the continuation of affirmative action programs for corporate America, with Congress voting the Armed Services even more money than they dared request; the navy, as a favor to the military contractors, will receive ships it does not want, the air force, planes it admits it does not need. Total federal subsidies to corporations are currently projected at about $265 billion over the next five years—exactly the sum the Republicans want to cut from Medicare. And the working or waiting poor are abandoned to a condition that no one, Republican or Democrat, even bothers to pretend will ever be alleviated by trickle-down benefits.

The dominant mood in America these days seems to be a viciously retributive one: thus we witness the reinstitution of the chain gang in Alabama, a bloodthirsty fervor for the death penalty, and the pending passage of a bill that would repeal Title 4A of the Social Security Act of 1935, which provides aid to dependent children—"the first time in the history of the nation," as Senator Daniel Patrick Moynihan of New York pointed out, "that we have repealed a section of the Social Security Act." Along with this comes a full-scale attack everywhere on public education, the liberal university, and scholarship in the humanities. I suppose it should have come as no surprise when, in late September 1995, it was announced that the National Endowment for the Humanities would offer no "Summer Stipends" for research in 1996.

It might well seem that the only avenue open to national pride these days is that of the bumper-sticker fantasy urging us to "Buy American"— a fantasy because almost any American-made item one might purchase is sure to contain components from Malaysia, Hong Kong, or Taiwan or to have been assembled in Honduras or Singapore or Bangladesh, so extensive has the transnationalization of production become. We not only can't answer Hector St. Jean de Crèvecoeur's eighteenth-century question "What is an American?" but also find it hard, now, to imagine just what such a question could possibly have meant.

Rejecting nationalism and, as well, what Richard Ohmann calls "the fatuous universalism of the right" (in Coiner 3), many have fallen back on—Ohmann's phrase again—"a politics of separate issues," an identity politics, as most usually conveyed by the familiar shorthand of gender-race-class, to which we presently add ethnicity and sexual preference. But as anyone can see, too narrow a focus on identity issues makes a broad-based movement for social change very difficult to envision, let alone achieve. In the same way, too narrow a focus on matters of identity hinders any attempt at a broad-based, progressive cultural criticism.

Emboldened by the splintered confusion of the dominant culture or, as it sometimes seems, mirroring it, some Native Americans have also sought to organize their concerns around identity issues, raising the question "Who is an Indian?" No one should deny the importance of this question—for all that granting it primacy is, in my view, an error. I mean only to point out that energies devoted to the task of defining identity are energies unavailable for the task of illuminating the larger question of just why it is that such definition seems so urgent. To preoccupy oneself with drawing the lines between "us" and "them" risks missing the sociopolitical and sociocultural issues around which (not quite all of) "us" and (at least some of) "them" might organize in common.

Nevertheless, it seemed to me that there was no responsible way to ignore identity questions in the criticism of contemporary Native literature. Self, subject, individual, person, agent, or mere occupant of a "subject position," each of us today finds her or his identity—American, Native American, gay, black, ethnic, working-class, or what have you—to be, in a more or less current terminology, a site of conflict: contested terrain. Thus I have addressed, in the chapters that follow, issues of identity. I have tried to conceive these issues broadly, and if I have been at all successful in elaborating them, they should bear on the interests not only of students of American Indian literature but also of a range of people engaged in a variety of historical and ethnographic inquiries as well: of all those concerned with intercultural criticism in whatever form.

I consider questions of critical identity—who may speak and whose "property" is being spoken about, for example—in the lengthy first chapter and, again, in the still-more-lengthy final chapter of this book. There I focus on what I think of as vocational identity, tracing my own personal history in order to suggest that who we *are* is an important function of what we *do*. An exercise in autobiography, and an act of self-definition, this final chapter may be seen as also linked to chapter 4, in which I study the autobiographical writing of Gerald Vizenor and read Vizenor's most recent novel, *Dead Voices* (1992), as fictional, to be sure, but "true" nonetheless, that is, as though it were also an act of self-identification, or an autobiography. I justify this reading with reference to various Native American perspectives on narrative truth and fiction as well as to Western perspectives on these matters, thus providing an example of what I have elsewhere called "ethnocriticism." I also look at Gerald Vizenor's work in my third chapter, where I examine his 1991 novel, *The Heirs of Columbus*, from the point of view of heritage or what Vizenor has called "heirship." Identity is also at issue here, for *The Heirs* offers a powerful meditation on the principles—*natio-* and *ratio-*, as I call them—by which communities may define themselves and so cohere and survive.

Chapter 2 looks at a number of contemporary Native American novels (and one piece of shorter fiction) in the context of postcolonialism.

These texts may, certainly, be considered among the postcolonial literatures of the world, and yet they are texts produced under conditions of
ongoing domestic colonialism. Suggesting first that these texts are best
identified as acts of what I call anti-imperial translation, I next' examine the ideological work these "translations" perform. Readers will no
doubt recognize other identitarian concerns in these chapters—as they will
also recognize that these concerns are not always central to the matters I
take up.

   This book offers itself as an active intervention in all those disciplinary
fields—some fairly new (American Indian Studies, Native American Studies, American Cultural Studies, Multicultural Studies, Ethnic Studies,
Postcolonial Studies) and some not so new (American Studies, American
Literature, English)—that might currently attend to contemporary Native
American literature. These are, of course, academic fields, and my intervention, such as it is, is an academic intervention. Nonetheless, I mean
these chapters to have not merely academic, but, in Edward Said's sense,
"worldly" implications, even—in however modest and indirect a fashion—
worldly effects. That is why I began this preface by attempting to situate my
own discourse in the world; it is also why—as the reader will soon see—I
take definite stands on a number of contested issues in the field. Although
I have tried to be "fair," for example, by offering the strongest version that
I can imagine of positions other than my own, I have not at all sought to
be "objective," to offer "balanced" accounts that aspire to some spurious
neutrality. I argue the case for my positions with the desire not so much
to be "right" as to present the clearest and most detailed accounting I can
for my views. This should help those who think differently to dispute me
on my own grounds or, indeed, to depart my grounds for others.

A different and briefer version of chapter 1, "Criticism and Native American Literature," appeared in *American Studies*, and I am grateful to the
editors for permission to reprint. Similarly, a shorter and somewhat different version of chapter 2, "Postcolonialism, Ideology, and Native American
Literature," after being presented before a conference titled "Ideology and
Esthetics" at Michigan State University, appeared in *Centennial Review*, to
whose editors thanks are due for permission to reprint. Chapter 3, "*Ratio-*
and *Natio-* in Gerald Vizenor's *Heirs of Columbus*," was first offered as a
talk at the University of Pennsylvania's conference on "Race in the Americas," and chapter 4, "*Dead Voices*, Living Voice: On the Autobiographical
Writing of Gerald Vizenor," was initially given as a brief talk for a Modern

Language Association convention panel in 1993. Neither has previously been published.

Chapter 5, "A Nice Jewish Boy among the Indians," also appears for the first time, and because it is rather different from the preceding chapters, perhaps a few more words about it here may not be amiss. My intention, as noted above, was to write a "vocational autobiography" (not, that is, a confessional or celebrational life history). I sought to explore possible linkages between my origins (as the son of working-class Jewish immigrants on the Lower East Side of New York) and my professional ends (as a teacher and critic of Native American literatures). In contrast to the mode of chapters that precede it, the mode here is predominantly narrative—for example, I tell a number of stories—even though there is no dearth of metanarrative, or criticism.

Notes to the first four chapters appear not at the back of the book but at the bottom of each page. Since most of the notes contain substantive material, it seemed important to me—in the interest of the reader's convenience and, too, in the interest of a certain dialogism (even though the dialogue is often with myself)—to present them in this fashion. But there are no footnotes for the book's last chapter, nor do any superscript numerals or parenthetical citations interrupt the narrative. Notes to "Nice Jewish Boy" can be found at the end of that chapter, providing documentation and occasional commentary.

A great number of friends have been kind enough to read and to comment on "Nice Jewish Boy" in one draft or another, and some of their comments are included in the text. In an earlier draft, I identified the authors of these comments by their initials; my intent was to make clear that—even though I was the one who got to decide whom and what to include—the inclusions represented real responses and they were not inventions of my own. But at the recommendation of my editor at the University of Nebraska Press, Doug Clayton, I have deleted the initials, bowing to the fact that they might tempt the reader to guess at the identity of the commentator and thus might detract, in some degree at least, from the substance of the comment. It seems appropriate here, however, to thank all those who were kind enough to read the text in one draft or another. I am very grateful to William Andrews, Donald Bahr, Betty Louise Bell, Bella Brodzki, Jane Campbell, Mary Ann Caws, Constance Coiner, G. Thomas Couser, Henry Giroux, Paul John Eakin, Dr. Gerald Hecker, Patricia Penn Hilden, tina, Dr. Harry Mendelsohn, Louis Owens, Roy Harvey Pearce, William Penn, Willis Regier, Julian Rice, Armand Schwerner, Amy Smiley, Brian Swann, Peter Whiteley, and Shamoon Zamir for their kind responses.

Thanks are also due my undergraduate research assistants, Matt Feivash and Michael Murray, for their help. I also gratefully acknowledge the assistance of the Sarah Lawrence College library staff, in particular Janet Alexander and Judith Kocinski.

THE TURN TO THE NATIVE

1

Criticism and
Native American
Literature

WHAT HAS SOMEWHAT MISLEADINGLY BEEN CALLED THE "NATIVE American Renaissance" in fiction, poetry, and autobiographical writing is usually said to have begun in 1968 with the publication of N. Scott Momaday's *House Made of Dawn*, a novel that won the Pulitzer Prize for 1969 and thereby brought contemporary Native American literature to the awareness of whatever "general public" for serious fiction might exist. Not surprisingly, this Native literary renaissance spurred something of a renaissance of critical writing about Native American literatures. Nor was it Momaday's substantial achievement alone that led to this latter development, for the year 1968 also saw the publication of Jerome Rothenberg's anthology *Technicians of the Sacred*, a book in which Rothenberg set the work of some European modernists in a context of a world poetry specifically concerned with the "sacred," offering a more-than-cursory selection from traditional Native American verbal performance. Inasmuch as all anthologies are inevitably acts of criticism, by their selection and arrangement of materials implying what their introductions and headnotes explicitly convey—a particular vision of a field, a particular set of values—Rothenberg's *Technicians* may be taken as initiating a new level of critical attention to the literary art of indigenous America.[1] From that

---

1. Though first and foremost in these regards, Rothenberg was certainly not alone. The

1

time forward, pioneering books and essays by Larry Evers, Karl Kroeber, Charles Larsen, Jarold Ramsey, A. Lavonne Brown Ruoff, Alan Velie, and Andrew Wiget among others have produced a new field of critical inquiry. What to call that field (American Indian studies, Native American literary criticism, Native American studies, and so on) is no mere matter of semantics—just as where to place that field institutionally, an issue I take up at the end of this chapter, involves more than formal or structural considerations.

With the field so undeveloped—with, perhaps, a post-1960s ecumenism still in effect at least in the academy—that early period now has the aspect of an "age of innocence," a time when it seemed not especially to have mattered that those establishing Native American literary criticism as a discipline were for the most part non-Natives. But perhaps that is only the fantasy of a non-Native like myself (and I was not "there" almost thirty years ago) rather than an accurate representation of "the way it really was." In either case, to invoke such a past today for longer than a sentence or two cannot help but raise the suspicion of a disreputable nostalgia for a prelapsarian world that could exist, as we know now, only so long as, to invoke the title of a recent and influential book, the empire did *not* write back. The critical world today, like the world in which people work and love and die, has changed; it is very much a place of "us" and "them." In our current "age of [bad] experience," we know it is not possible to proceed without some reference to one's own "positionality" or "social location": the instantiation of personal bona fides as being one of "us," the offer of apologetic admission for being one of "them." To write criticism of ethnic or "minority" literatures today (to write anything at all!) without an awareness of the many significant issues gathered under the little words "us" and "them" is to write (as Canon Kingsley said of Cardinal Newman) as either a knave or a fool; and one would, of course, prefer to be neither. Thus the opening and closing chapters of this book attend closely—here a bit more "objectively," there a bit more "subjectively"—to questions of critical identity, a kind of tentative mapping of what might constitute my

---

poets Gary Snyder, Armand Schwerner, and others were very seriously engaged with Native American materials in these years, and the founding of the journal *Alcheringa* in 1970 by the anthropologist Dennis Tedlock and the poet Rothenberg, with the early aid of the Acoma poet Simon Ortiz, helped to bring Native American literary expression to a wider American audience. Some of these developments have been traced by Michael Castro's *Interpreting the Indian*, a volume that—along with these developments themselves—has been criticized as more nearly appropriating the Indian. To the best of my knowledge, the first college course in Native American literature was Alan Velie's at the University of Oklahoma in 1970.

own, or any other critic's, grounds for speech, of my relation, as it were, to critical culture.

This introductory chapter began as a response to Daniel F. Littlefield Jr.'s presidential address to the Middle America American Studies Association, published in 1992 as "American Indians, American Scholars, and the American Literary Canon." That account of the state of Native American literary studies sought to bring into the open what Littlefield saw (accurately, I think) as the field's growing factionalization, with Native and non-Native critics beginning to operate as "us" and "them." Although this focus permitted a great many questions to be raised in a brave and timely manner, it nonetheless seemed to obscure a good deal more than it clarified—and yet, as I have noted, there seemed then and seems now no way in good faith *not* to confront questions of critical identity. I offer here five somewhat arbitrary and often overlapping headings for my remarks, substantially revised and very much expanded from their first appearance; these issues seem to me still urgent.

I begin with a strong critique of what might simply be called the problem of essentialization, along with its consequence, my second category, the problem of the double bind. I move next to the issue of Native sovereignty, a term that still refers to the realms of law and politics even though it has been given a definite cultural inflection, such as in the notion of "intellectual sovereignty" or "autonomy." My account here too is critical, although—as I hope all through this chapter and this book—it is a constructive criticism that I offer. This is the case as well for the fourth category I take up, the matter of cultural property, usually presented interrogatively in terms of the question "To whom does culture 'belong'?" I conclude with a consideration of the possible institutional placements for the criticism of Native American literatures in the age of multiculturalism.

The Problem of Essentialization

Much debated in African American studies, in women's studies, and most recently, in various considerations of "postcoloniality," essentialization— the tendency to specify racial, cultural, or (much less frequently) class traits as fixed or given and as largely determining discursive practice—has become implicit to some extent in Native American literary studies, where it has only begun to be theorized explicitly.[2] It seemed to me that Littlefield

---

2. Cook-Lynn's 1993 essay "Cosmopolitanism, Nationalism, The Third World, and

tended toward essentialization, for example in his approval of the notion that Indian "journalism organizations . . . develop . . . guidelines for non-Indian journalists who write about Indians" (101), without the slightest sense that if such guidelines were indeed useful, then Indian journalism organizations might also want to extend them to Indian journalists who write about Indians.

Feminists know perfectly well that to be born a woman is not necessarily to be a feminist; African American scholars do not always agree simply because the dominant culture classifies them all as people of color. In the same way, to be Indian—whatever the (vexed) criteria for Indianness might be—provides no guarantee of any particular journalistic or scholarly or critical perspective or expertise. As T. S. Eliot wrote in "Dry Salvages," "We had the experience but missed the meaning." It is always possible to have the experience but miss the meaning—or to offer meanings that others who have had the same or virtually the same experience would contest. To know that a particular scholar is a white male is not necessarily to know what he thinks—about white males, about Indians, or about anything else. The case is the same if a particular scholar is an Indian, male or female.

Wendy Rose, who is both a Native poet and an anthropologist, wrote that when she is "called upon to speak anthropologically," she finds herself "apologizing or stammering that [she is] not *that* kind of anthropologist" (408). She means this both in a disciplinary sense—that she is a quite humanistically oriented anthropologist—and, I believe, in a moral and political sense: she is not the kind of anthropologist who has been the bane of Native Americans for more than a century. But of course today there are a fair number of non-Native anthropologists who are "not *that* kind of anthropologist" either. The issue is not strictly whether you are a Native or a non-Native anthropologist but what *kind* of anthropologist you are.[3]

Tribal Sovereignty" remains the strongest and best account of the "nationalist," "nativist," and anti-"cosmopolitan" position. I find it inaccurate on several counts (for example, in its understanding of the "Indian Nationalism" of Leslie Marmon Silko's *Almanac of the Dead*) and, as will be readily apparent below, mistaken in its logic and its estimate of possible outcomes. But no supporter of the internationalist or cosmopolitan position should proceed without taking Cook-Lynn's arguments into account.

3. In rather confusing fashion, the newly opened Museum of the American Indian at the old Customs House in lower Manhattan both recognizes and ignores this fact. Viewing the exhibits in the recommended order, one initially finds items with the following captions: "the view of art history," "the anthropological view," and "the Native view." One then comes upon overhead panels called "The Native View" and "The View of Anthropology," set directly opposite one another. The art history and the anthropology views are chosen from rather stiff and ethnocentric sources. But the first statement of "the Native view" I recall is

I want it to be clear that in offering thus far what is a fairly standard critique of essentialization, I am *not* arguing against generalization, nor even against certain forms of totalization. Social and political analysis of a nontrivial sort cannot proceed by attention to an infinite number of incomparable and unique particulars, so generalization is both unavoidable and necessary. Thus it is entirely legitimate to invoke the category of "American Indians" as a historically and geographically specific indigenous population and of "Euramericans" as a historically and geographically specific population of colonist-settlers; general statements can most certainly be made about both groups in spatial and temporally specific terms. What I am arguing against is the essentialized version of the general, the type of statement that is *not* historically and geographically specific in its assumption that to *be* an Indian (whatever that may mean) is always and everywhere to be this, that, or the other foreknown and fixed thing, that to *be* of European background (whatever that may mean) is to be this, that, or the other foreknown thing. How "long . . . it take[s] to *become* indigenous," as James Clifford notes ("Diasporas" 309), is always a political question, but surely Native people have claims to firstness as Americans.

Nonetheless, historical indigenousness is not the same as mythical autochthony: there is no *essence* of America that Native people automatically incarnate, just as there is no *essence* of Europe (or elsewhere) inherent in people or groups with near or distant ties to those places. This is why there can be no guarantee that Indian journalists will write "better" or more accurate or more sympathetic stories about Indians than will non-Indian journalists.

It is not my intention in any way to deny the importance (or the lived reality) of the experience of being Indian; rather, I am trying to insist on the obvious fact that Indian experience is not always and everywhere the same, nor is it ever unproblematically given to consciousness (nor is consciousness unproblematically represented in writing). *All* experience must be interpreted, and even people who have the "same" experience (the quotation marks indicate the differences inevitable in any "sameness") may interpret it differently, reaching very different conclusions about what their experience means and the uses to which that meaning may be put in any attempt to understand Native American culture, history, and literature.

The essentialist position posits an experiential plenitude and similitude

---

from a Chippewa poem in a "translation" by Armand Schwerner, a Jewish American from Belgium who does not know the Chippewa language. Later sources for the native view come from no less than Claude Lévi-Strauss and a number of anthropological sources.

for all those people marked *X*, and thus, as my remarks mean to show, it is logically untenable and, historically, simply false or at the very least unverifiable. To leave the matter at that, however, would be, as Ruth Frankenberg and Lata Mani have written, "to aggrandize theory, while failing to grasp the complex and contradictory workings of power/knowledge" (301). Frankenberg and Mani note, with sympathetic intent, "The legitimacy of land-rights claims of indigenous or Fourth World peoples turns on ahistorical conceptions of culture and essentialist notions of identity" (301). This account of the matter is hardly transferable to the Native American situation, in which specific treaty rights, failed contractual commitments, and outright fraud can be instantiated as thoroughly historical and nonessentialist "claims" for lands. Nonetheless, as Ella Shohat has pointed out, it is quite clear that some assertions of culture and, here, identity "prior to conquest" are essentialist assertions; they are rhetorical acts in the interest of a material-political "regeneration" (110). These rhetorical acts are, obviously enough, performed for their practical effectiveness rather than for their logical coherence or factual accuracy. Thus anyone who operates as a progressive worldly intellectual is likely to find himself or herself at some point saying, with Kwame Anthony Appiah, "I am enough of a scholar to feel drawn to truth telling, *ruat coelum*; enough of a political animal to recognize that there are places where the truth does more harm than good" (175). But here I hope it will not be amiss to speak, if only briefly, to the distinction between philosophy ("truth telling," logic, dialectic) and rhetoric.

Although no one today can have any illusions that dialectic can be rigorously distinguished from rhetoric, it is still possible to believe, as Peter Hulme wrote, not in "a transcendental Truth," but in "a small and relative and provisional truth," one that "claims an explanatory superiority over its rival versions, particularly since it includes within its analysis an explanation of why those rival claims might appear plausible" (8). This sort of truth—decentered, qualified, and relativized—may be approached by rational and logical procedures that are not strictly "Western" or "Eurocentric" but panhuman.[4] In what follows I will do my best to argue logically and rationally. As a non-Indian, I perhaps have that luxury; as a

---

4. I say this in full knowledge that my criteria for "truth" are nonetheless culturally and historically determined, deriving ultimately from the Enlightenment. Other modes of producing and living knowledge are certainly felt as equivalently "truthful" by those who produce and live those ways. I have wrestled more fully—if in the end, I must admit, less than successfully—with this issue in "American Histories, Native American Stories." See also Marvin Harris's much-attacked but nonetheless valuable arguments (in, for example, *Cultural Materialism*) for a panscientific social science.

non-Indian, I also have that responsibility. This is *not* to claim innocence in regard to the political implications of even the aspiration to truth or dialectic; rather, it is to say, with Jean-Paul Sartre (see his *Anti-Semite and Jew*), that there is some correlation between a relatively secure social position and the possibility of philosophy.

But even as I try to show that some of the arguments offered by some Native American scholars have more rhetorical than logical force, I do so in a spirit of solidarity and support—hoping, of course, that the notion of critical support is not taken as a contradiction in terms. It is clear enough that those Native Americans who assert their "Indianness" as authorizing them to define and comment on Native American culture do so in order to improve the prospects for Native people. Cultural politics are not, as some have said, politics by other means; they are real politics carried on at what an older Marxism would have called the superstructural level and what a post-Althusserian Marxism might call the ideological level— all those places where power and knowledge meet. How could oppressed people not feel the need to produce knowledge in the interest of some small gain in power—to argue at times rhetorically, whatever the logic?

We can point to some statistics here that would seem to confirm the necessity of rhetoric, the felt urgency to argue "by any means necessary." In 1986, for example, minorities accounted for 22.4 percent of American high school graduates; of these, only 0.7 percent were American Indian. American Indian and Alaskan Natives in 1986 received only 0.4 percent of bachelor's degrees in all fields, by far the lowest percentage of all minority groups (*Digest of Education Statistics, 1990* table 235). Also, "Despite progress in 1992, American Indians earned only 0.5% of all degrees at the associate, bachelor's, masters, and first-professional levels" (Carter and Wilson 20). After a steady growth in the number of doctorates earned by Native people in the years 1983–92, "American Indians experienced a sudden decline in the number of doctorates they earned in 1993"—119 nationwide, with only 13 of these in the humanities (Carter and Wilson 24–25). I have figures by fields within the humanities only for 1989–90, when just 0.1 percent of the doctoral degrees granted to American Indians were in the field of English and American literature, with another 0.3 percent in modern foreign languages (American Council on Education).[5]

---

5. This would seem to be inconsistent with the figures given by Michael Pavel, Karen Swisher, and Marlene Ward in their "Special Focus: American Indian and Alaska Native Demographic and Educational Trends," in Carter and Wilson, *Minorities*. For 1990, these authors give a total of 96 doctorates granted to American Indians and Alaska Natives; 0.1 percent

Not surprisingly, "fewer than one in 200 full-time faculty members [at colleges and universities in the United States] was an American Indian in 1991, *the same proportion as in 1981*. Overall, American Indians continued to represent only 0.3% of all full-time faculty"(Carter and Wilson 32, my emphasis). Most of these Native American faculty members are "concentrated in the disciplines of communications and education." Of faculty in all fields, "American Indians accounted for only one of every 500, or 0.2 percent, of full professors in higher education in 1991" (Carter and Wilson 32).

These figures make it abundantly clear that an ongoing domestic colonialism has been quite successful in keeping the Native American population from the "benefits" of higher education. Indian academics, particularly at the highest levels, are very few and must surely feel embattled. It is no wonder that the line between dialectic and rhetoric tends to shift and blur as Native scholars "fight back," in Simon Ortiz's phrase, in whatever way they can "for the people."

Nevertheless, when M. Annette Jaimes wrote, in the introduction to her collection of essays called *The State of Native America*, that because most of the contributors to the book were Native Americans they could "be said to speak with an 'Indian voice,'" (10) one must pause. Is there such a thing as "an 'Indian voice'" in the singular? In what would that voice consist? How would one know it when one heard it? Of the Native contributors to Jaimes's book, Jimmie Durham does not sound like Wendy Rose; neither of them sounds like John Mohawk, and both of them on occasion sound at least a little bit like Jim Vander Wall, a non-Native contributor. If some Native American or I were to read passages from the works of these and other Native and non-Native scholars, I doubt whether Jaimes or anyone else would be able to guess which authors were Native and which non-Native. To assert the existence of "an 'Indian voice'" discernible in critical writing, is to argue rhetorically, not logically.

It should not be thought that my objections to the positing of a unitary and essentialized "Indian voice" (which implies a unitary and essentialized "non-Indian voice") or my insistence that the quality or value of a thought not be taken as wholly determined by the race, gender, or culture of the thinker means to deny the importance of location or positionality.

---

of that figure would be less than a single doctorate granted in English and American literature. The discrepancy is almost surely due to different computational methods. The article by Pavel, Swisher, and Ward is indispensable reading for an understanding of these issues.

No thought occurs in a vacuum, and of course it is important to take into account the formation of the speaker. I will speak to my own formation at some length in the final chapter of this book. Who one is and where one speaks from, as Linda Alcoff has made clear in an important essay called "On the Problem of Speaking for Others," are indeed "epistemically salient" (7). But who one is (identity) and where one speaks from (location) mean "*social* location, or social identity," and social locations and identities are plural, complex, and constructed. Identities are not—as in the essentialized Native/non-Native opposition—unitary, simple, and fixed or given in advance. Thus the various aspects of any particular person's identity may be, as Alcoff explains, socially empowering or disempowering.

In these regards, it is not immediately clear, for example, whether a white male who speaks from Florida Atlantic University is more or less privileged than an Indian male who speaks from Stanford or UCLA. Does it change things if the white male is Jewish or if one of the Indian males is part-Jewish and currently (1995) the chairman of his tribe? In an essay called "The Unauthorized Autobiography of Me," Sherman Alexie offers "An Incomplete List of People Whom I Wish Were Indian." Among the thirty-three people on Alexie's list are Voltaire, Patsy Cline, Meryl Streep, and Walt Whitman. Isn't it at least possible to imagine that Alexie (or some other Native writer) might produce a list (undoubtedly not for publication!) of people he or she wished were *not* Indian? What is the oppressor/oppressed equation when Native American women defend a Native man against charges of sexism raised by non-Native women, or when Indian women raise the issue of sexism on the part of Indian men? Is a lesbian Indian scholar at a triple disadvantage in relation to white, male, "straight" scholars? Questions of this sort might easily be multiplied; and there are no easy answers to them. The point, however, is that these questions are always pertinent, so that reliance on essentialized categories like Native/non-Native is an obstacle to real critical work. Any answer to the question "Who speaks?" does not automatically convey the kind and quality of the speech.

Still, in the same way that one would not want to see the criticism of literature by women and African Americans largely in the hands of men or Euramericans, so too criticism of the literature of Native Americans should not be largely in the hands of non-Native people. Nor will it be: that is a political necessity, and I dare say it is a historical inevitability; in ten years, five years, a little more or a little less, Native people *will* be in the majority of those engaged in the criticism of Native American literature, history, and culture. Native people should mostly be determining the criticism of Native literature not only for political reasons but also because that is the situation that approaches the ideal case. So long as it is indeed *criticism* that is involved—once more, not strictly narrative but metanarrative, a discourse *about* stories more nearly than a story—what is most desirable in the critic is a combination of the fullest knowledge (e.g., of a theoretical, historical kind) and the fullest experience relevant to the subject at hand. Non-Natives as well as Native people can attain to whatever abstract or "book" knowledge is necessary to any given critical task regarding Native American literature, but only Native people can attain to anything approximating full experience.

Thus, for all my insistence that Indian "experience" is not monolithic, not always and everywhere the same, there is no doubt that Native people have a variety of experiences that differ from (many of) those of non-Native people and that make them more likely to be sensitive, aware, in touch with the experiential dimension of a variety of Native texts in a way that non-Natives (like myself) simply can't be. My class experience, for example, as the last chapter will indicate, parallels that of many Native people, but there is surely a cultural sensibility, different yet the same among different Native people, that I do not and cannot have. So Native people *should*, I think, even beyond politics (is there such a thing as beyond politics?), be in the majority in the criticism of Native literature because they can approach the ideal of intellectual and experiential adequacy in a way that non-Native critics (and that group certainly includes me) cannot. But to say that is *not* strictly the same thing as saying that Indians, simply by being Indian (and I note again that what it means to be Indian is not always and everywhere the same thing), are automatically and inevitably the best people to consult for every task involving the interpretation and understanding of Indian history, literature, and culture.

To return to the point I made earlier, even though essentialist positions on identity are logically untenable, "so long as other conceptions of identity have effectivity in the world, we necessarily need to engage them" (Frankenberg and Mani 301). Given that "ahistorical conceptions of culture" (Frankenberg and Mani 301) often serve as rhetorical gestures in the interest of justice, a rigid antiessentialist position may indeed be reactionary. Thus it will be necessary for positions of "anti-antiessentialism" or "strategic essentialism" to be worked out as complex ways of negotiating the rhetorical demands of the essentialist position and the dialectical demands of the antiessentialist position. Useful here, perhaps, is Paul Gilroy's commitment to "'the changing same,' something endlessly hybridized and in process but persistently there—memories and practices of collective identity maintained over long stretches of time" (in Clifford, "Diasporas" 320).[6] To quote Appiah once more, "We cannot change the world simply by evidence and reasoning, but we surely cannot change it without them either" (179). Abandoning "evidence and reasoning" for an essentialist identity politics leads, pedagogically at least, to our next category.

The Problem of the Double Bind

Double binds are situations in which you're damned if you do and damned if you don't. They are logically untenable and, to those who experience them, practically intolerable. It is illogical and intolerable, for example, for non-Native scholars to be excoriated when they fail to include Native American materials in their teaching and writing on American history, culture, and literature and also to be excoriated when they do include them, on the grounds of colonial appropriation, "speaking for others," experiential inadequacy, or inauthenticity.

If, as Phillip S. Deloria has claimed, a failure to be critical of Indians smacks of arrogant and critically blind romantic idealization (in Littlefield 96) but an intense critique of Indian self-identifications—for example, in some of the work of James Clifton—is dismissed in toto as "racist," then we have a potential double bind.[7] For a Native scholar to denigrate the work of a prominent non-Native scholar by suggesting (mistakenly, as it happens) that the non-Native has probably never been to a powwow and then to publish remarks ridiculing non-Indians at powwows is to set up a double bind.[8]

---

6. Clifford's discussion links Gilroy's "black Atlantic" to the position of anti-Zionist, prodiasporic Jews like Daniel and Jonathan Boyarin—with passing reference to indigenous Americans. I consider aspects of this linkage, with reference to my own experience, in the final chapter of this book.

7. To my knowledge, Ward Churchill has been more guilty of this sort of thing than any other critic, Native or non-Native, as in his ad hominem attacks on James Clifton, Werner Sollors, and Sam Gill, among others. For Churchill, there is no such thing as critical disagreement; there is only betrayal, bad faith, and so on. A cursory glance at the essays collected in Churchill's *Fantasies of the Master Race* will provide more than ample evidence for this assessment.

8. Elizabeth Cook-Lynn in the *Lakota Times/Indian Country Today*, November 5, 1992. See also the letter protesting her remarks as racist in the December 3 issue and the letter protesting their characterization as racist in the December 31 issue.

To take seriously the advice of many Native scholars that if America is to survive, it had better learn something from the Indian—and then find a wide range of attempts to learn categorized as intellectual tourism, cultural imperialism, or the imposition of an unjust burden on the Indian—is to find oneself in a double bind. Native critiques of the *kinds* of inclusions Native and non-Native scholars may make, of the *kinds* of critiques offered, and of the *kinds* of information requested are always appropriate. But so far as it is scholarship or criticism—the production of knowledge about a practice—that is at issue, there are neither ethical nor epistemological grounds for condemning inquiry on the basis of its source or origin.

I can most efficiently convey my sense of the ethical issue by turning to Satya Mohanty's recent discussion of Kantian "universalism." Mohanty cites Kant's *Foundations of the Metaphysics of Morals*, where Kant wrote, "Now, I say, man and, in general, every rational being exists as an end in himself and not merely as a means to be arbitrarily used by this or that will" (in Mohanty 117). Mohanty comments that the Kantian claim "concerns a basic capacity shared by all humans. . . . Hence it is perfectly compatible with different ways of particularizing and specifying discrete situations and the kinds of additional rights and entitlements those situations call for" (117). For our present purposes, I read this as consistent with my argument that whereas Native critics may, on occasion or often, be particularly well-positioned, as a result of their experience, to produce certain kinds of knowledge, there is no ethical ground for excluding a priori the "universal" aspiration to knowledge of any "rational being," all such beings existing equivalently as human ends-in-themselves. The knowledge aspired to, of course, is once again "knowledge" as defined by the rationalist-secularist paradigm of the Western Enlightenment. But the Native American scholars whose work I know seem, in their publications, largely to be playing by these rules—even though those from traditional backgrounds may sometimes operate according to very different cognitive paradigms.

Nonetheless, so far as we are indeed talking about critical knowledge, there are also epistemological reasons for not excluding anyone, a priori, from making a contribution. For efficiency's sake, let me make my brief demonstration of this point by citing James Clifford's phrase "partial truths" (Clifford and Marcus passim). Clifford's phrase points to the fact that the "truths" any one of us can individually offer are inevitably "partial" in the sense of partisanship (e.g., we are all *partial* to certain views) as well as in the sense of incompleteness (e.g., we can never see more than a *part* of what there is to be seen). If we are insiders to the events or the experiences we wish to observe, our understanding benefits from closeness and familiarity. But it is just that closeness and familiarity that may preclude a certain still-valuable measure of dispassionate distance and "objectivity." (Too much distance, of course, may cause one simply to miss the point or misunderstand.) To continue with the obvious, it should be clear that we are each at every moment inside and outside of some experiences and some knowledges and that any aspiration to expand that part of the truth we may grasp needs the perspectives of both insiders and outsiders—in this case, those of a range of Native people and those of a range of non-Native people.

Not to see this is to perpetuate an intolerable double bind for both Native and non-Native students of Indian literature, culture, and history. For Native critics, the impossible situation concerns the fact that when they speak as insiders, they may be seen as lacking in academic "objectivity," yet when they speak "objectively," from the outside, they may be seen as having abandoned their people or their experientially privileged position. For non-Native critics, as I said at the outset, their experiential distance from the phenomena in question may be taken as disqualifying, and their attempts to approach nearer may be seen as arrogance and impertinence. In all cases, this is to be avoided.

Political Sovereignty, Cultural Sovereignty, Autonomy

My understanding of the issue of political sovereignty for Native Americans derives substantially from Vine Deloria Jr. and Clifford Lytle's 1984 study, *The Nations Within: The Past and Future of American Indian Sovereignty*. Deloria and Lytle offer a cogent distinction between Indian self-government and Indian self-determination, this latter largely synonomous with what is meant, today, by Native sovereignty.

Self-government for Native Americans is the product of the 1930s and the tenure of John Collier as President Franklin Roosevelt's commissioner of Indian affairs. The concept is predicated on a desire to extend Euramerican conceptions of civil rights and entitlements to Indians. This desire, although generally benevolent in its intentions, is nonetheless misguided because it is based on a mistaken understanding of the cohesive principles of Native American societies. As Deloria and Lytle make clear, "traditional Indian society understands itself as a complex of responsibilities and duties" (213), in contradistinction to "modern" Euramerican societies in which specific civil rights written into law stand protectively between the people and the state or government. In traditional, small-scale Native societies, because all members are bound by kin or clan ties, the concept of abstractly defined and legally codified civil rights is essentially meaningless.

Native societies, thus, do not conceive of themselves in any manner equivalent to Euramerican states or governments (e.g., with generalized and abstract notions of law, right, and justice). Rather, Native societies conceive of themselves as nations, where the nation is not the modern nation-state but a synonym for the people (who, to repeat, have specific and concrete relations, entailing responsibilities). It is nation-to-nation relations as people-to-people relations that are thus particularly meaningful to Native Americans.

Native Americans have good historical reasons for believing that nation-to-nation relations of this sort were also important to the U.S. citizens, who, immediately after winning their own independence from Britain, negotiated treaties with the tribes as one sovereign nation to another. It is this treaty relation that, according to Deloria and Lytle, is "the spiritual but not the practical heritage of Indians" (10). It is not "the practical heritage of Indians" because it is not now, and for long has not been, the way in which the federal government has operated toward Native people.

Yet this heritage of sovereignty is not only spiritual but also legal-historical, a matter not only of the past but also of the fairly recent present. It is traceable from opinions of Chief Justice John Marshall in the nineteenth century to Solicitor Nathan Margold's "Powers of Indian Tribes" in 1934 (Deloria and Lytle: "Modern tribal sovereignty . . . begins with this opinion" [158]), to the 1977 Abourezk Commission's Report, which affirmed that "Indian tribes are sovereign political bodies" (Deloria and Lytle 228). Deloria and Lytle see the 1972 Indian March on Washington and its important if too-often neglected document, the Twenty Points, as initiating the contemporary Indian focus on the restoration of the treaty relationship between the United States and the tribal nations and thus on Native sovereignty.[9]

---

9. The Twenty Points (or demands) appears in the *Hearings of the Committee on Interior and Insular Affairs of the House of Representatives* for December 4 and 5, 1972, along with the government response to the Twenty Points. In the early winter of 1973 a special issue of *Akwesasne Notes* devoted to the Trail of Broken Treaties March on Washington and the takeover of the Bureau of Indian Affairs also published the Twenty Points. A slightly condensed version, along with the government response, and a "Reply" to the government by Vine Deloria Jr. appear as an appendix to the clothbound edition of Deloria's *God Is Red*. I am grateful to Vine Deloria for helping me track down the Twenty Points. The debate between Native American leaders and the government centers on the government's determination to treat Indians as individuals (and thus to resist Indian demands on the basis of the argument that the United States does not make treaties with its citizens) as against the Native position that Indians should be dealt with collectively as sovereign nations. In addition, the Twenty

It is not for me to say what should or might happen between the federal government and the tribes in these regards. I think it is, however, reasonable to say that whatever happens, it is unlikely that Native American nations, in any foreseeable future, will possess sovereignty in anything like the literal dictionary definition of that word. The *American Heritage Dictionary*, third edition (1992), gives the following meanings for *sovereignty*:

> 1. supremacy of authority or rule as exercised by a sovereign or sovereign state. 2. Royal rank, authority of power. 3. Complete independence and self-government. 4. A territory existing as an independent state.

The second and fourth definitions seem inappropriate to the Native American context, the second definition for obvious reasons, the fourth inasmuch as even nineteenth-century proposals for the creation of an Indian state never assumed that this state might be any more independent (i.e., a *nation*-state) of the federal government than were any of the existing states. Definitions one and three seem more likely as referents for contemporary Native aspirations to sovereignty, although here too "supremacy" of rule and "complete" independence are hardly realistic likelihoods. Lest this seem to denigrate Native Americans' desire in these regards, it should be said that in the present moment of transnational capitalism, no state or nation has sovereignty in the strong sense of the dictionary definition. Even the United States is subject to the requirements of multinational corporatism, as, for example, in the instance of American economic policy toward Mexico, a policy largely determined by the need to bail out Citibank. Mexican "sovereignty," meanwhile, like the "sovereignty" of all developing nations, is thoroughly compromised by the demands of the World Bank and the International Monetary Fund.

It may be, then, that Chief Justice Marshall's description of the tribes in *Cherokee Nation v. Georgia* as "dependent, domestic nations," may today, as Vine Deloria has written, mean that "the Indian tribes of this country stand on the same footing with respect to the United States as does Monaco toward France, San Marino toward Italy, and Liechtenstein toward Switzerland and Austria" (329). Even were this to be admitted by the

---

Points calls on the United States to treat Native peoples fairly while also insisting that Native Americans are not to be treated as just another ethnic group. Complex as the reasoning may be here, it is nonetheless perfectly correct because the United States is in fact established on Native—not Polish or Chinese or Italian—land. The Native position tends to be perceived as contradictory (how can you be fair and still give special treatment to Indians?) by the mainstream population, for all that it is historically accurate.

federal government, Indian self-determination would still be constrained by the Congress and courts of the United States and by a variety of state and federal bureaus and agencies—perhaps only (or even) to the extent, as Deloria notes, that "Switzerland administers Liechtenstein's currency, telegraph and postal service, and its foreign affairs" (329).

In this regard, legal sovereignty and cultural sovereignty—to get to this matter at last—although they may seem to be digital (on/off, either/or, you have it or you don't), are in fact more nearly analogue (loud/soft, hot/cold, more or less).[10] Both political sovereignty and cultural sovereignty are meaningful only contextually and conjuncturally. In the first instance, sovereignty is the material outcome of negotiations on a variety of levels between Native American tribes or nations and a multiplicity of non-Native institutions and governmental entities. In the second instance, sovereignty is yet again the result of complex negotiations and encounters between traditional cultural practices and the practices, impossible to circumvent or ignore, of Euramerican cultures.

Thus when M. Annette Jaimes criticizes scholarly journals and academic presses for not undertaking "American Indian Studies efforts per se" and calls for "an autonomous *Indian* tradition of intellectualism" (in Littlefield 98), it is hard to know just exactly what is meant. What are Indian studies "per se"? The Latin phrase itself denies the meaning of what it would convey: what is an "autonomous *Indian* tradition of intellectualism" "per se"? I am not looking to score easy points; I am simply offering an example of the way some contemporary Native American discourses committed to cultural sovereignty, cultural autonomy, or cultural separatism, in an apparently absolute sense, readily subvert themselves—even, as here, in the very texture of the language they use. Jaimes again provides an example of this when she speaks for "the articulation of native American perspectives *vis-à-vis* the content of various disciplines and without adherence to the academic structures specific to those disciplines (e.g., Native American philosophy is philosophy in its own right, and not by virtue of a juxtaposition to the philosophy of Plato or Hegel)" (in Littlefield 106). Apart from the "*vis-à-vis*" and, again, the Latin "e.g." (*exempli gratia*, for the sake of example), where might one find "Native American

---

10. A good deal of confusion about these matters derives from what John Tomlinson calls "UNESCO discourse" (70) with its insistence that "cultural autonomy is inseparable from the full exercise of sovereignty" (72). As Tomlinson shows in detail, this slogan, admirable on the face of it, is marked by all sorts of misunderstandings and contradictions. See Tomlinson, *Cultural Imperialism*.

philosophy . . .in its own right"? The same is true for Littlefield's claim that "American Indian literature is literature in its own right, not by virtue of its juxtaposition to American literature" (106).

I need again to emphasize that my point is in no way to deny the existence of such things as Native American philosophical thought then— whenever "then" would be, pre-Columbus, usually—and now. But "Native American philosophy" is a Western category, and so is "Native American literature." So too "Native American religion" and "Native American art" are Western categories. Traditional cultures abound in philosophical thought, powerful verbal and visual expression, and deeply felt relations to the divine or supernatural. But traditional cultures neither conceptualize nor linguistically articulate the generalized abstract categories of philosophy, literature, and religion. Indeed, the absence of such categories has frequently been asserted not as a lack but as a positivity: Native cultures were holistic, unified, integral. Of course they did not rigidly separate the esthetic, religious, or philosophical dimensions of human experience, one from another. But you cannot logically make this case *and* also ask that Native "philosophy" or "literature" be studied "in their own right."

Further, to restate the obvious, Native philosophical and religious thought and Native literary expression are available for study and commentary only insofar as they exist in texts. And Native American writing, whether in English or in any indigenous language, is in itself testimony to the conjunction of cultural practices, Euramerican and Native American; it is inconsistent with any claim to a radical cultural independence or autonomy.

Anthony Appiah has challenged the African "nativist" to specify "the content of [his] injunction to read literature by means of a theory drawn from the text's own cultural or intellectual inheritance" (65). And Elizabeth Cook-Lynn has forthrightly acknowledged that it *is* "the challenge of modern thinkers and critics to find out what . . . nativist ideals mean in terms of the function of the literature" ("Cosmopolitanism, Nationalism," 31).[11] Until that is done, calls to a "nativist" criticism can have only

---

11. Until very recently, this "challenge" was met predominantly by anthropologists and linguists (e.g., Donald Bahr, Keith Basso, William Bright, Nora and Richard Dauenhauer, Michael Foster, Leanne Hinton, Dell Hymes, Geoffrey Kimball, Toby Langen, Alfonso Ortiz, William Powers, Blair Rudes, David Shaul, Dennis Tedlock, and many others)—whose work was not necessarily inspired by a commitment to "nativism." Of late, Native and non-Native literary scholars, whatever their views on "nativism," have begun to respond to Cook-Lynn's call. At the 1995 Modern Language Association convention, a good half dozen papers listed in the program promised work in this direction.

rhetorical force; indeed, when that is done (as I believe it will be), even a focused "nativist" criticism will not have the sort of radical autonomy or sovereignty now claimed for it.

Parallel to Jaimes's desire to posit an "autonomous *Indian* tradition of intellectualism" is Terry Wilson's 1979 concern to base Native American studies on "a uniquely American Indian perspective" (in Willard and Downing 2). Again, one must wonder in what such a uniqueness could actually consist. One may fantasize that in the history of the Americas, Columbus's three little boats sank shortly after setting out, but the fact remains that from 1492 on, neither Euramerican intellectuals nor Native American intellectuals could operate autonomously or uniquely, in a manner fully independent of one another, for all the differences in power relations. It is much the same thing when Robert Warrior calls for more attention to the work of the Indian intellectuals John Joseph Mathews and Vine Deloria Jr. in the interest of advancing the cause of "intellectual sovereignty." But surely the thought of Mathews and Deloria can no more be understood without reference to the Euramerican tradition than can Warrior's. Further attention to Mathews and Deloria and to, perhaps, John Milton Oskison, Francis LaFlesche, Gertrude Bonnin, and a great many other formidable Native American intellectuals might, at this historical juncture, be more important than continued attention to any of a number of non-Native intellectuals. But to consider these Native thinkers as "autonomous," "unique," "self-sufficient," or "intellectually sovereign"—as comprehensible apart from Western intellectualism—is simply not possible. Nor, if it were possible, would it be useful for the purposes claimed. As Appiah has poignantly written, "For us to forget Europe is to suppress the conflicts that have shaped our identities; since it is too late for us to escape each other, we might instead seek to turn to our advantage the mutual interdependencies history has thrust upon us" (72). As a non-Native critic, I once more find it impossible to say what "we" should do; as a critic committed to the study of Native American literature, I can only state my belief that Appiah urges us in the right direction.

The discussion above, I hope it will be clear, means not to dismiss out of hand the commitment to cultural autonomy of Jaimes, Wilson, Warrior, and a number of other Native intellectuals but rather to situate it. As Ella Shohat has powerfully noted, "The assertion of culture prior to conquest forms part of the fight against continuing forms of annihilation" (110). It is a fight that is ongoing in many parts of the world, not only in the Americas. Native scholars are among those who, once more in Shohat's words, feel themselves "obliged by circumstances to assert, for their very survival, a lost and even irretrievable past" in the interest "of their own regeneration" (110) and the regeneration of their people, attempting, in the phrase of the Kenyan novelist Ngũgĩ wa Thiong'o, to "decolonize the mind." Although it seems impossible to deny that power/knowledge and rhetoric/dialectic are always everywhere intertwined, I hope it may still be possible to claim—again, for I have made this claim above—that they are not always and everywhere the same, that specific discursive gestures can be tentatively shown to bear, now more nearly the mark of a will to truth, now more nearly the mark of a will to power. It is in the interest of knowledge, then, that I have offered a critically supportive account of those commitments to cultural autonomy that I see as in the (justifiable) interest of power, hoping all the while that what Marx called "critique" can itself help not merely to understand the world but to change it.

Cultural Property: To Whom Does Culture "Belong"?

I can get at this issue most directly by considering Robert Warrior's rejection of what he sees as my wish to have "Native American literature 'belong' to the national literature of the United States" (in Littlefield 105). I have indeed taken the position that Native American literatures should be *included* among the many literatures that make up American literature and that American literature itself should be *included* in the broader category of a global or international literature, what I have called a "cosmopolitan" literature. But I nowhere use the word "belong" in the sense that Warrior attributes to me. (Warrior cites no page reference.) Is this carelessness or opportunism on his part? Littlefield, quoting Warrior approvingly, affirms that "the literature [Native Americans] produce does not 'belong' to America" (105)—as if anyone but Warrior had suggested that it might.

William Willard and Mary Kay Downing accurately quote what I have said on this matter: "Indian literatures ought to be included in the canon of American literature so that they might illuminate and interact with the texts of the dominant, Euroamerican culture, to produce a genuinely heterodox national canon" (in Willard and Downing 2). But clearly what I call inclusion means possession for Warrior, and apart from setting the record straight, I want to use his conflation of the two nouns to get at the question "To whom does culture 'belong'?" As my title for this section indicates, it is a question that currently forms itself around the phrase "cultural property."

To whom does Native American literary culture "belong"? Warrior would probably answer (Littlefield, a more temperate thinker, seems undecided) that Native American literatures "belong" to Native Americans, who retain or should retain (individually, collectively, "nationally"?) primary if not exclusive rights to possession and use. This sort of cultural nationalism has, in the past, been challenged by a kind of humanist universalism that insists, in the words of Jaime Litvak King, that "cultural property is not, and cannot be claimed to be, the absolute property of a nation, any one nation. It is the property of humankind as a whole" (in Messenger 212). But I think neither of these positions is useful for the subjects of my particular concern: literary criticism and Native American literature.

The cultural property debate in its current form arose in the 1970s as a result of concern for the fate of material objects taken from the third, or less-developed, world to—for the most part—the United States. It has involved archaeologists, customs officers, diplomats, art dealers, private collectors, museum officials, lawyers, and judges.[12] Its terms have included such things as cultural patrimony or heritage, national sovereignty, public or scholarly access, rescue and preservation, and definitions of "legal" possession or, as the *McClain* decisions of 1977 and 1979 specifically addressed the matter, what it means to say that cultural objects have been "stolen."[13]

It is also possible, as Karen Warren has written, to conceive "the debate over 'cultural properties' . . . as a debate over ownership of the past," where "the past" is "understood not only as the physical remains of the past (e.g., artifacts, places, monuments, archeological sites) but also the 'perceptions of the past itself' (e.g., information, myths, and stories used in reconstructing and transmitting the past)" (in Messenger 2). Here we begin to approach nearer to our particular concern: information and stories, or literary criticism and Native American literature. Yet, as Warren continues, "for persons in a cultural context where 'the past' is not viewed as property, perhaps, not even as 'past' (e.g., some Native American cultures), or where talk of property, ownership, utility, and rights do not capture important conceptions of the past (e.g., communal kinship with the 'living

---

12. The earliest American book I have found on the matter is Karl Meyer's *The Plundered Past* (1973), a loosely constructed journalistic and anecdotal account that nonetheless, in its many appendices, offers useful statistics and documents.

13. As Douglas Ewing construes it from the point of view of the art dealer, the conclusion to be drawn from *McClain* is that "any Pre-Columbian objects entering this country from whatever source and under whatever circumstances were presumed to have been stolen" (in Messenger, *Ethics of Collecting*, 180). Although that may be excessive (and self-serving), *McClain* seems most certainly to have broadened the notion of "stolenness" very considerably in regard to the movement of art and artifacts from poor nations to rich ones. The issues raised in my discussion above can all be explored in Messenger, *Ethics of Collecting*.

past'),'" to persist in using a language of property, even for information and stories, is to perpetuate misunderstandings (in Messenger 15). How, then, are we more appropriately to speak of these matters?

I can only suggest a turn to what I have elsewhere called an "ethnocritical perspective." Such a perspective begins by recognizing the differences between Native American and Western conceptions of art, information, and culture in general and attempting, next, to find some language that might mediate between the two. Here one seeks to avoid hierarchical models and to employ what Warren calls "compromise" or "consensus" models (in Messenger 17). One might, for example, note the fact (a "fact" only, of course, at a high level of generalization) that indigenous peoples have tended to believe that all members of society have a right to a portion of its material goods but that only certain members of society have a right to its informational goods or knowledge. One might then note, by way of contrast, that the modern, capitalist West has tended to believe (or, at least, to state as an ideal) that all members of society have a right to information but that only certain members of society (those who are productive, the "fittest," and so on) have a right to its material goods. The West has prided itself on this commitment to free inquiry or open access, even though many of us now see it as an imperial excuse for overriding others' desire *not* to be "known" or simply to keep some information—ceremonials, rituals, songs—within culturally prescribed limits.[14] We have tended not to notice or to care much about what David Sassoon has called the "devastation" in indigenous America and elsewhere "caused by the foreign [Western] imperative to study, catalogue, and collect" (in Messenger 89)—and, one might add, in academic circles, to publish. As Peter Whiteley noted, "Dissemination of ritual knowledge, either orally to unentitled parties or *ipso facto* in published accounts, violates ritual sanctity and effectiveness and may damage the spiritual health of the community" (139).

To say this, however, is not to affirm the largely rhetorical commitments I have criticized above invoking cultural sovereignty or cultural autonomy. In varying degrees, all verbal performances studied as "Native American literature," whether oral, textualized, or written, are mixed, hybrid; none are "pure" or, strictly speaking, "autonomous." Native American written literature in particular is an intercultural practice; moreover, so far as it

---

14. But as Peter Whiteley has noted in "End of Anthropology," "Secrecy, particularly regarding instrumentally powerful knowledge, is, of course, a universal social practice." For all of our "trumpet[ing] an unproblematized version of 'free speech,'" we have nonetheless "produced multiple secret praxes in military and other matters" (139n).

is written for publication, it is offered to a general audience, all of whose members in their own ways "receive" it, even though none of them can in any reasonable way be said to "own" it. Native American people may feel a special relation to Native American literature and feel this relation as conferring a particular authority to speak of it, but contemporary Native American literature is a practice, not a thing, and as a practice, it cannot "belong" either to American literature or to (some rhetorically constituted) Native American literature "in its own right."

This is true as well for a good deal of oral literature. Once there is a degree of circulation of stories, that is, once narrators permit "outside" auditors to record, translate, and publish stories, then—again—although "insiders" may be especially well positioned to speak of these stories, there is no ground on which they can claim sole rights to possession.[15] People with different sociocultural identities and different social locations will have different relations to these materials, and these relations may indeed cause them to speak about and represent the materials differently. But it remains to be said yet again that one cannot know, a priori, the nature and force of any given person's speech and representation.

For all of these reasons, the cultural property metaphor for most of what is taken as Native American literature obscures far more than it clarifies, and this is the case even for those textualized oral performances of a sacred or traditionally circumscribed kind that probably never should have been transcribed, translated, and published in the first place. Rather than say that certain stories and ceremonials, along with certain artifacts, "belong" to particular lineages of storytellers, clans, or people, acceding to a language of commodity and possession, it seems better to refer to these people or groups as the culturally sanctioned guardians, stewards, or "friends" of the materials. I refer here once more to Whiteley, who wrote, "For Hopis, even the concept 'mask,' implying representational falsity, in itself violates the items' sanctity. In English Hopis usually refer to [masks] as Kachina 'friends' (translating from the Hopi reference *ikwaatsi*, 'my friend'), actively avoiding 'mask' (129n). Hopis and other friends and guardians of cultural artifacts and knowledge act not so much as their producers as their transmitters. I will try briefly to elaborate my understanding

---

15. There are, of course, a good many instances of published materials that are rather like "stolen" objects in that the people who have made the materials public have acted without consulting their producers or caretakers or have acted against their expressed wishes. Is there a way in which it would prove useful to speak of "repatriating" stories or ceremonial language, as one currently speaks of repatriating a range of material objects?

of the distinction between the production and the transmission of knowledge, readily admitting that I feel better qualified to speak to what literary critics or ethnographers are doing than to what traditional Native Americans are doing. In any case, this is an exercise in heuristics, an attempt at cultural *translation*.[16] I am trying to find Western concepts and English terms to approximate my best guess at what people who work with different conceptual paradigms and languages are about.

All those engaged in critical scholarship—intellectuals, literary critics, and so on—whatever their genetic, geographic, or cultural backgrounds, are all *producers* of knowledge. Littlefield, Jaimes, Warrior, and I, among others, select from an ever-increasing number of resource materials what we find of interest or value, interpreting those materials and producing a discourse about them. To use again the title of a well-known collection of essays, we "write culture," and in this case, the "culture" we write is called literary criticism.

In the case of ritual and ceremonial knowledge, "culture" is not, of course, written; nor is it produced. Rather, it is transmitted. Although traditional culture does not remain static, the changes in it and the circulation of it are so organized as to remain relatively fixed. To wrench such knowledge from its prescribed transmissional circuits, thus opening it to the unlimited circulation of produced knowledge, is a violation of trust and propriety, and actions to prevent such violation constitute legitimate exercises of sovereignty. Consider, for example, recent Hopi attempts to keep a book on the sacred salt journey off the shelves or to recall an issue of Marvell comics.[17] Here, I think, neither censorship (the great cry "Foul!" of the West) nor cultural possession (this knowledge "belongs" to the Hopis) adequately names what is at issue. In these particular instances, the Hopis, who have themselves neither published such knowledge nor produced it in substantial interaction with the knowledges of the dominant culture, have strong claims to control as—again—its exclusive or privileged guardians, stewards, or friends. This situation, as I have tried to show, differs substantially from the scholarly production of knowledge focused on Native American literature as a cultural practice. In all cases involving literary criticism and Native American literature, we do best to avoid reference to

---

16. For more on cultural translation, see below.

17. The issue of Marvell comics for March 1992, entitled *NFL Superpro*, in Whiteley's description "featured the steroid-inflated superhero" pitted against "named Hopi Kachinas" ("End of Anthropology," 139). This was not an instance of inaccurate representation; rather, the very fact that the representations *were* fairly accurate was the problem.

cultural property and to arguments determined to show what "belongs" to whom.

I will conclude this section by briefly noting the way in which "cultural property" of the sort I have been discussing has come to be conflated with the recent term "intellectual property." Mainstream debates about "intellectual property" concern newly created materials—software, information on the Internet, and the like—in regard to which legal "ownership" is claimed as a necessary condition for profit. The corporation or individual deemed to be the "owner" of the "intellectual property" at issue may take pride in the fact that "ownership" also means something like what "authorship" once meant, but the main issue is *money*.

A 1995 document issued by the "Hopi Tribe Office of Historical and Cultural Preservation and Protection" states, "The Hopi people desire to protect their rights to privacy in and to Hopi intellectual property . . . so as to protect the rights of the present and future generations of the Hopi people" (n.p.). The document continues, "The Hopi Tribe reserves the right to *not* sell, commoditize or have expropriated from them certain domains of knowledge or information" (n.p.). Here we find the older sense of "cultural property" (control of the transmission of knowledge handed down from the past) carrying over into the newer term "intellectual property" (control of the production of knowledge as a salable commodity). The Hopi use of "intellectual property" in the document I have cited is clearly a necessary strategic move under current conditions. My own discussion is meant both to acknowledge the importance of strategic responses to current conditions and to clarify the complexities and nuances of those conditions that strategic responses may obscure.

Native American Literary Studies
In The Era of Multiculturalism

Everyone knows that cultural conservatives like Allan Bloom, William Bennett, Lynne Cheney, and the egregious Jesse Helms, among others overtly or covertly committed to the primacy of the traditions of Europe and America, are opposed to what is generally—if not always clearly or consistently— termed multiculturalism. But champions of the vitality and integrity of Native American traditions are not necessarily in favor of multiculturalism. Evelyn Hu-DeHart opens Annette Jaimes's book with a preface in which she states her wish that "Eurocentric parochialisms" would yield "to the more inclusive pluralistic project," a project she names multicultural. Yet Hu-DeHart accurately notes that the one theme that "runs explicitly through each of the contributions [in Jaimes's collection] . . . is that of indigenous demands for sovereignty, self-determination, and self-sufficiency" (x)—demands, so far as they are meant in the strong sense, that are simply not compatible with multiculturalism.

Thus, the mixed-blood Cherokee painter, poet, and activist Jimmie Durham wrote, "Institutions in the United States are already reinforcing racism by celebrating 'multiculturalism.' " This celebration, he continued, "makes intervention on [Native Americans'] part more difficult" (in Jaimes 426)—difficult in that, as I imagine (Durham doesn't quite say), the multicultural project offers a modicum of cultural equality as a substitute for social, economic, and political equality. Or, as Martine Charlot wrote, "The right to difference is a concession the majority grants to certain minorities . . . on the condition that hierarchical relationships remain intact. The right to difference never results in equality" (88, my translation). In these regards, it must be noted that whatever multiculturalism may be in the academy, it is, in the wider world, the cultural logic of transnational capitalism. What is one to think when "tenured radicals" find themselves in unexpected strategic accord with the *Harvard Business Review?* Nonetheless, along with many other progressive academics, I am on record as being "for multiculturalism," in the hope that its pedagogical and critical strategies might contribute to a breakdown of "hierarchical relationships" and to a cosmopolitan vision that would stand against age-old narrow sectarianisms and endless bloody battles between "us" and "them" not only in the academy but in the world, and not just the world of transnational capital.[18]

In my view, multiculturalism is best understood as a critical and pedagogical strategy. That is, the term loses its force when used as a vague synonym for *diverse* or *complex*—as, for example, when one says that Americans eat a "multicultural" diet (e.g., egg rolls, bagels, pizza, burritos, etc.) or that New York is a "multicultural" city (e.g., it has a population that includes Haitians, Taiwanese, Puerto Ricans, Pakistanis, Koreans, etc.). As I have argued in my *Ethnocriticism*, multiculturalism on the pedagogical level implies the sociopolitical values of cosmopolitanism. But, as I have noted, multiculturalism and cosmopolitanism have been opposed by some Native American critics whose pedagogical startegies make claims to cultural "sovereignty" and "autonomy," the political implications of which strategies are nationalistic. I will not take the time here to explain the

---

18. See, for example, the conclusion to my *Ethnocriticism*.

ways in which the multicultural-cosmopolitan orientation and the cultural sovereignty–nationalist orientation can have a good deal in common.[19] Instead, I want to consider where the multicultural-cosmopolitan and the cultural sovereignty–nationalist scholar might best place himself or herself in the American academy.

The cosmopolitan critics might aspire to teach Native American literature in specifically multicultural programs, although there are few enough of these at present (and whether there will or should be more is not at all clear). American Studies or American Cultural Studies departments or programs might also prove congenial as a home for the cosmopolitan critic of Native American literature, and there may be room as well in certain broadly conceived Cultural Studies programs. The nationalist critic might prefer to locate the teaching of Native American literature in independent American Indian Studies and Native American Studies departments or programs or in an Ethnic Studies department or program.

Thus, Mario Garcia, whose work is in the area of Chicano or Latino studies, argues that American studies and ethnic studies need to come together "to negotiate a new type of intellectual popular front or a new form of historical bloc, one based on an equal and democratic relationship" (55). In more or less parallel fashion, Patrick Morris has called for Native American studies "to be intellectually broad and integrative, utilizing all academic disciplines and methodologies to search, identify and address the critical issues relevant to the Native Community" (in Willard and Downing 2). William Willard and Mary Kay Downing speak of "American Indian/Native American Studies [as] preparing the way toward intercultural education" (1), with their term "inter-cultural" being synonomous with most uses of multicultural. I think Jaimes has moved to something like this position as well, for near the end of her introduction to *The State of Native America* she wrote, "Despite the fact of our coming from different traditions, we are now singing to the same drum, locked together in our common humanity and our common destiny" (10). But some still hold to Russell Thornton's 1978 concern to see "Indian Studies as a separate discipline" (in Willard and Downing 6). The Lakota novelist and educator

---

19. The multicultural critic sees cosmopolitanism as the furthest horizon of cultural and political possibility in the interest not only of independence but of human liberation. (For more on this, see the discussion of Frantz Fanon in chapter 5.) This is indeed a utopian position, where "utopian" does not mean materially unachievable Platonic ideals, or daydreams, but rather a model beyond the currently real. I offer a full account of these matters in a forthcoming essay "Nationalism and Cosmopolitanism in the Criticism of Native American Literature."

Elizabeth Cook-Lynn, for example, is on record as wanting Indian studies to exist as an "alternative regime of intellectual thought . . . not only through content but through methodology" ("Radical Conscience" 11). For Cook-Lynn, the "integrity" of Native American studies can be maintained only by its disciplinary separation from multicultural or American studies. She asserts, "The integrity of what we do comes from the sober understanding of, and the regulating, and defending of the parameters of that discipline" ("Radical Conscience" 11).

I disagree with this view because I believe it to be both flawed in its logic and mistaken in its assessment of practical possibility. But I take it very seriously. How could Native Americans *not* be wary of an aggressive majority's sudden invitation to come in and share, the offer of an inclusion that might well be just another way to appropriate, absorb, and nullify? Cook-Lynn, in the essay from which I have quoted above, insists that worries about the possible ghettoization of Native American Studies programs that insist on their separateness or "autonomy" from multicultural, ethnic, or indeed American Studies programs are just a way of trying to keep Indians from doing things their own way. And it would be naive to pretend there isn't something to that.

But a commitment to separatism, as Joan Wallach Scott has written, "is a simultaneous refusal and imitation of the powerful"(71). Because our histories are entwined, "no group is without connection or relation to any other, even if these are hierarchical, conflicted, and contradictory relations" (75). To deny this is to practice what Fernando Coronil calls "Occidentalism," a "complex ensemble of representational strategies engaged in the production of conceptions of the world that a) separates its components into bounded units; b) disaggregates their relational histories; c) turns differences into hierarchy; d) naturalizes these representations; and therefore e) intervenes, however unwittingly, in the reproduction of existing asymmetrical power relations" (in Turner 18–19). Of course it remains to be seen if in practice as well as in theory we can indeed achieve community without homogeneity, what Scott refers to as "communities of difference" (76).

The major difference between scholars committed to a separate Native American studies curriculum and their more inclusionist colleagues is not, I believe, a difference of content or methodology but rather one of purpose. (Here I am talking of scholars, Native or not, who work within a secular critical paradigm, a "Western" paradigm, if you will, but one that has pan-human possibilities. My comments do not apply to scholars and teachers at, for example, Navajo Community College or Sinte Gleska, who work within a religious paradigm: the Navajo or Lakota "way.") In Patrick Morris's words, "It is [a] definitive commitment to the Native community and people, rather than to academics alone, that distinguishes Native American Studies from other academic disciplines" (in Willard and Downing 2). Certainly Native scholars will feel this "commitment" more powerfully and immediately than will most non-Native scholars,—although I suspect that not many non-Native scholars in this field would admit to being committed to "academics alone."[20]

Finally, then, my own sense of the best location for the criticism of Native American literature is for it to be situated *both* in Native American Studies/American Indian Studies programs *and* in American Cultural Studies/American Studies programs. This is, of course, consistent with the notion that the production of knowledge about Native American literatures is usefully sited among both "insiders" and "outsiders." In the same way, Native American literatures should be strongly represented in American literature courses—and there should as well be specific courses devoted to the "Oral Tradition," the "Native American Novel," and so on.

Louis Owens has wittily noted "the current tendency of critics to consider Bakhtin as a topical ointment applicable to virtually any critical abrasion," adding that "Bakhtinian analysis strikes [him] nonetheless as a valuable tool" (Other Destinies 256). It is Mikhail Bakhtin that I too would invoke to suggest that a "dialogic" approach to the issues I have been discussing may well be useful. To take Bakhtin's thought seriously— and I won't take the time to detail what that would mean in the present context—is to go beyond a vague pluralism or an untheorized commitment to diversity to a recognition that *our* speech and thought is inevitably implicated in the speech and thought of others. Postcolonial work on Native American history, culture, and literature cannot help but occur in what Mary-Louise Pratt has called "contact zones" (4ff), even though we have tended to think of "contact zones" as somewhere "out there" rather than just "here," close to wherever we think of as home. Work on the "borders"—as defined by Guillermo Gomez-Peña, Ramón and José David Saldívar, and others—will manifest itself in some form of what I myself have called "ethnocriticism."

In our attempts to produce an ethnocriticism today, we are in something like the situation Leon Trotsky described in his *Literature and Revolution*. That is, we can't hope adequately to theorize such work short of its real

---

20. Native scholars may well feel more powerfully the need to reconcile, so far as possible, the secular paradigm within which they work with the religious traditionalism that they all seem to respect.

existence in practice—but we can't hope to bring it into practice without first attempting its theorization. In this situation, we will need the "negative capability" described by a writer very different from Trotsky: the poet John Keats. We will need the ability to rest with doubts, uncertainties, and dim intuitions. This is not a prescription for passivity; rather, it is an exhortation—the politics of criticism having mostly hortatory status—to stay calm and stay committed, to distinguish between rhetoric and logic so far as possible, and to value both truth and power.

2

Postcolonialism, Ideology, and Native American Literature

IN THE CURRENT CLIMATE OF LITERARY STUDIES, IT IS TEMPTING TO think of contemporary Native American literatures as among the postcolonial literatures of the world. Certainly they share with other postcolonial texts the fact of having, in the words of the authors of *The Empire Writes Back*, "emerged in their present form out of the experience of colonization and asserted themselves by foregrounding the tension with the imperial power, and by emphasizing their differences from the assumptions of the imperial centre" (Ashcroft, Griffiths, and Tiffin 2). Yet contemporary Native American literatures cannot quite be classed among the postcolonial literatures of the world for the simple reason that there is not yet a "post-" to the colonial status of Native Americans. Call it domestic imperialism or internal colonialism; in either case, a considerable number of Native people exist in conditions of politically sustained subalternity. I have remarked on the academic effects of this condition in the first chapter; here I note the more worldly effects of this condition: Indians experience twelve times the U.S. national rate of malnutrition, nine times the rate of alcoholism, and seven times the rate of infant mortality; as of the early 1990s, the life expectancy of reservation-based men was just over forty-four years, with reservation-based women enjoying, on average, a life-expectancy of just under forty-seven years.[1] "Sovereignty," as I have tried to explain in the preceding chapter, whatever its ultimate meaning in the complex sociopolitical situation of Native nations in the United States, remains to be both adequately theorized and practically achieved, and "independence," the great desideratum of colonized nations, is not, here, a particularly useful concept.

Arif Dirlik lists three current meanings of the term *postcolonial*. Postcolonial may intend "a literal description of conditions in formerly colonial societies," it may claim to offer "a description of a global condition after the period of colonialism"—what Dirlik refers to as "global capitalism," marked by the "transnationalization of production" (348)—and it may, most commonly in the academy, claim to provide "a description of a discourse on the above-named conditions that is informed by the epistemological and psychic orientations that are products of those conditions" (332). Is any one of these meanings useful to describe contemporary Native American literature?[2] Dirlik's first sense of the postcolonial will not work because, as already noted, the material condition of contemporary Native "societies" is not a postcolonial one. His second sense might perhaps come a bit nearer, inasmuch as Native societies, although still in a colonial situation, nonetheless participate in the global economy of a world "after the period of colonialism." To give a fairly undramatic anecdote, in Santa Fe Native Americans sell traditional ceramic work and jewelry (including "traditional" golf tees) across the street from where non-Native people offer the "same" wares made in Hong Kong. In something of a parallel fashion, Lakota people travel to Germany and Switzerland to promote tourism at Pine Ridge. As for the last of Dirlik's definitions, little discourse surrounding Native American literature, to the best of my knowledge, has been self-consciously aware of having been formed "by the epistemological and psychic orientations that are products" of the postcolonial. (And the "nationalist" Native critic seeks to reject any formation whatever according to these "orientations.") Perhaps, then, it may not be particularly useful to conceptualize contemporary Native American literature as postcolonial.

---

1. Alan Velie has pointed out to me that these statistics should not lead to the general conclusion that all Native American are "victims" enmeshed in the "culture of poverty." In Oklahoma, for example, there are a great many oil-rich Natives; in Connecticut, the Mashantucket Pequots number among the super-rich.

2. I again refer the reader to Cook-Lynn, "Cosmopolitanism, Nationalism," for a discussion of these matters from a "nationalist" perspective.

But even though contemporary Native American fiction is produced in a condition of ongoing colonialism, some of that fiction not only has the look of postcolonial fiction but also, as I will try to show in the second part of this chapter, performs ideological work that parallels that of postcolonial fiction elsewhere. Here, however, I want to suggest a category—the category I will (again) call anti-imperial translation—for conceptualizing the tensions and differences between contemporary Native American fiction and "the imperial center." Because historically specifiable acts of translative violence marked the European colonization of the Americas from Columbus to the present, it seems to me particularly important to reappropriate the concept of translation for contemporary Native American literature. To do so is not to deny the relationship of this literature to the postcolonial literatures of the world but, rather, to attempt to specify a particular modality for that relationship.

To say that the people indigenous to the Americas entered European consciousness only by means of a variety of complex acts of translation is to think of such things as Columbus's giving the name of San Salvador to an island he *knows* is called Guanahani by the natives—and then giving to each further island he encounters, as he wrote in his journals, "a new name" (in Greenblatt 52). Columbus also materially "translated" (*trans-latio*, "to carry across") some of the Natives he encountered, taking "six of them from here," as he remarked in another well-known passage, "in order that they may learn to speak" (in Greenblatt 90). Columbus gave the one who was best at learning his own surname and the first name of his firstborn son, translating this otherwise a-nonymous person into Don Diego Colon.

Now, any people who are perceived as somehow unable to speak when they speak their own languages, are not very likely to be perceived as having a literature—especially when they do not write, a point to which we shall return. Thus, initially, the very "idea of a [Native American] literature was inherently ludicrous," as Brian Swann has noted, because Indian "languages themselves were primitive" (xiii). If Indians spoke at all, they spoke very badly (and, again, they did not write). In 1851, John De Forest, in his *History of the Indians of Connecticut*, observed, "It is evident from the enormous length of many of the words, sometimes occupying a whole line, that there was something about the structure of these languages which made them cumbersome and difficult to manage" (in Swann xiii). Difficult for *whom*, one might ask, especially in view of the fact that De Forest himself had not achieved even minimal competence in any Native language. Further, inasmuch as these were spoken languages, not alphabetically written languages, any estimate that single words occupied the length of "a whole line" could only depend on De Forest's decision to write them that way. De Forest's sense of the "cumbersome and difficult" nature of Indian languages, as I have noted, implies that any literature the Natives might produce in these languages would also be "cumbersome and difficult." Perhaps the Natives would do better to translate themselves or be translated, to "learn to speak"—in this case, to speak English—in order to have a literature. De Forest was wrong, of course, although what most people know as Native American literature today consists of texts originally written in English.

Almost half a century after De Forest, as late as 1894, Daniel Brinton—a man who actually did a great deal to make what he called the "production" of "aboriginal authors" visible to the dominant culture—nonetheless declared, "Those peoples who are born to the modes of thought and expression enforced by some languages can never forge to the front in the struggle for supremacy; they are fatally handicapped in the race for the highest life" (in Murray 8). The winners in the "race for the highest life," therefore, would be the race with the "highest" language; and it was not the Indians but rather, as Brinton wrote, "our Aryan forefathers" who were the ones fortunate enough to be endowed "with a richly inflected speech." As Kwame Anthony Appiah explained in reference to Johann Gottfried von Herder, the *Sprachgeist*, "the 'spirit' of the language," is "not merely the medium through which speakers communicate but the sacred essence of a nationality. [And] Herder himself identified the highest point of the nation's language in its poetry" ("Race" 284), in its literature. "Whoever writes about the literature of a country," as Appiah elsewhere cited Herder, "must not neglect its language" (50). For those like the Indians with "primitive" languages, there would seem to be little hope, short of translation, for the prospects of literary achievement. Thus, by the end of the nineteenth century, the linguistic determinism expressed by Brinton—and, of course, by many others—worked against the possibility of seeing Native Americans as having an estimable literature at exactly the moment when the texts for that literature were, for the first time, being more or less accurately translated and published.

But here one must return to the other dimension of the translation issue as it affects Native American literatures. For the problem in recognizing the existence of Native literatures was not only that Natives could not speak or, when they did speak, that their languages were judged deficient or "primitive" but also that they did not write.

Here I will only quickly review what I and others have discussed elsewhere.[3] Because *littera-ture* in its earliest uses meant the cultivation of letters (from Latin *littera*, "letter"), just as *agriculture* meant the cultivation of fields, peoples who did not inscribe alphabetic characters on the page could not, by definition, produce a literature. (They were also thought to be only minimally capable of agriculture in spite of overwhelming evidence to the contrary, but that is another story.) It was the alteration in European consciousness generally referred to as "romanticism" that changed the emphasis in constituting the category of literature from the medium of expression, writing—literature as culture preserved in letters—to the *kind* of expression preserved, literature as imaginative and affective utterance, spoken or written. It is only at this point that an oral literature can be conceived as other than a contradiction in terms and the unlettered Indians recognized as people capable of producing a "literature."

For all of this, it remains the case that an oral literature, in order to become the subject of analysis, must indeed first become an object. It must, that is, be textualized; and here we encounter a translation dilemma of another kind, one in which the "source language" itself has to be carried across—*trans-latio*—from one medium to another, involving something more than just a change of names. This translative project requires that temporal speech acts addressed to the ear be turned into visual objects in space, black marks on the page, addressed to the eye. Words that had once existed only for the tongue to pronounce now were to be entrusted to the apprehension of the eye. Mythography, in a term of Anthony Mattina's, or ethnopoetics has been devoted for many years to the problems and possibilities involved in this particular form of media translation.[4]

Translation as a change of names—as a more or less exclusively linguistic shift from "source" to "target" language—may, historically, be traced in relation to the poles of identity and difference, as these are articulated within the disciplinary boundaries of what the West distinguishes as the domains of art and social science. Translators with attachments to the arts or humanities have rendered Native verbal expression in such a way as to make it appear attractively literary by Western standards of literariness,

---

3. Cf. in my "Native American Literature and the Canon," *The Voice in the Margin*, and my essay "On the Translation of Native American Literature: A Theorized History," in Swann, *On the Translation*. See also Cheyfitz, *Poetics*, in these regards and Murray, *Forked Tongues*, in particular chapter 1, "Translation," and chapter 2, "Languages."

4. For a recent overview, with particular attention to Iroquois and Navajo examples, see Zolbrod's *Reading the Voice*. My own essay "On the Translation of Native American Literature" offers bibliographical references to most of the efforts at mythography or ethnopoetics.

thereby obscuring the very different standards pertaining in various Native American cultures. Conversely, translators with attachments to the social sciences have rendered Native verbal expression in as literal a manner as possible, illuminating the differences between that expression and our own but thereby obscuring its claims to literary status. I have elaborated on these matters elsewhere,[5] and so I will here turn from considerations of the formal implications of translation practices to their ideological implications. I want to explain what I mean by anti-imperial translation and why it seems to me that a great many texts by Native American writers, though written in English, may nonetheless be taken as types of anti-imperial translation.

I base my sense of anti-imperial translation on a well-known, indeed classic text, one that I have myself quoted on a prior occasion.[6] The text is from Rudolph Pannwitz, who is cited in Walter Benjamin's important essay "The Task of the Translator." Pannwitz wrote:

> Our translations, even the best ones, proceed from a wrong premise. They want to turn Hindi, Greek, English into German instead of turning German into Hindi, Greek, English. Our translators have far greater reverence for the usage of their own language than for the spirit of the foreign works. . . . The basic error of the translator is that he preserves the state in which his own language happens to be instead of allowing his language to be powerfully affected by the foreign tongue. (in Benjamin 180–181)

My use of Pannwitz was influenced by Talal Asad's paper "The Concept of Cultural Translation in British Social Anthropology," originally presented at the School for American Research in 1984 and published in James Clifford and George Marcus's important collection *Writing Culture* in 1986.[7] As will be apparent, I am much indebted to Asad's work.

Asad's subject, like mine, is not translation in the narrow sense but rather translation as cultural translation. The "good translator," Asad wrote, "does not immediately assume that unusual difficulty in conveying the sense of an alien discourse denotes a fault in the latter, but instead critically examines the normal state of his or her *own* language" (157). Asad notes the fact that languages, if expressively equal, are nonetheless politically "unequal," those of the third world that are typically studied by

---

5. See Krupat, "On the Translation of Native American Literatures," in Swann.

6. See Krupat, *Ethnocriticism*, 196–99, 237.

7. A somewhat different version of this paper was presented by Asad and John Dixon in July 1984 at the University of Essex's "Sociology of Literature" conference. This version appears as "Translating Europe's Others," in volume 1 of the proceedings of the conference, *Europe and Its Others*.

anthropologists being "weaker" in relation to Western languages (and to-day especially in relation to English).[8] Asad remarks that the weaker, or colonized, languages "are more likely to submit to forcible transforma-tion in the translation process than the other way around" (157–58). Asad cites with approval Godfrey Lienhardt's essay "Modes of Thought" and quotes Lienhardt's exemplary explanation of anthropological translation: "We mediate between their habits of thought, which we have acquired with them, and those of our own society; in doing so, it is not finally some mysterious 'primitive philosophy' that we are exploring, but the further potentialities of our thought and language" (in Asad 158–59). This sort of translation, Asad affirms, should alter the usual relationship between the anthropological audience and the anthropological text, in that it seeks to disrupt the habitual desire of that audience to use the text as an occa-sion to know *about* the Other, a matter of "different *writings and readings* (meanings)" in order to instantiate the possibility that translation, as a mat-ter "of different *uses* (practices)" (160), can be a force moving us toward "*learning to live another form of life*" (149).

My claim is that Native American writers today are engaged in some version of the translation project along the broad lines sketched by Asad. Even though contemporary Native writers write in English and configure their texts in apparent consonance with Western or Euramerican literary forms—that is, they give us texts that look like novels, short stories, po-ems, and autobiographies—they do so in ways that present an "English" nonetheless "powerfully affected by the foreign tongue," not by Hindi, Greek, or German, of course, and not actually by a "foreign" language, inasmuch as the "tongue" and "tongues" in question are indigenous to America. The language they offer, in Asad's terms, derives at least in part from other forms of practice, and to comprehend it might just require, however briefly, that we attempt to imagine living other forms of life.

This is true of contemporary Native American writers in both literal and figurative ways. In the case of those for whom English is a second lan-guage (Luci Tapahonso, Ray Young Bear, Michael Kabotie, Ofelia Zepeda, and Simon Ortiz are some of the writers who come immediately to mind), it is altogether likely that their English will show traces of the structure and idioms of their "native" language, as well as a variety of linguistic habits and narrative and performative practices of traditional expressive forms in

---

8. In this regard, see John Tomlinson's discussion (in *Cultural Imperialism*) of the lin-guistic imperialism resulting from the fact that even anti-imperial discourse takes place only in a very few languages, English *primes inter pares*.

Navajo, Mesquakie, Hopi, Tohono O'odham, and Acoma.[9] Their English, then, is indeed an English, in Pannwitz's words, "powerfully affected by the foreign tongue," a tongue (to repeat) not "foreign" at all to the Americas. Here the Native author quite literally tests "the tolerance of [English] for assuming unaccustomed forms" (Asad 157), and an adequate commentary on the work of these writers will require of the critic if not bilingualism then at least what Dell Hymes has called some "control" of the Native language.

Most Native writers today are not, however, fluent speakers of one or another of the indigenous languages of the Americas, although their experiences with these languages are so different that it would be impossible to generalize. (E.g., Leslie Marmon Silko certainly heard a good deal of Laguna as she was growing up, just as N. Scott Momaday heard a good deal of Jemez, whereas many of the Native American writers raised in the cities did not hear indigenous languages on a very regular basis.) Yet all of them have indicated their strong sense of indebtedness or allegiance to the oral tradition. Even the mixed-blood Anishinaabe—Chippewa— writer Gerald Vizenor, someone who uses quotations from a whole range of contemporary European theorists and whose own texts are full of ironic effects possible only to a text-based literature, has insisted on the centrality of "tribal stories" and storytelling to his writing.[10] This is the position of every other contemporary Native American writer I can think of: all of them insist on the storytelling of the oral tradition as providing a context, as bearing on and influencing the writing of their novels, poems, stories, or autobiographies.

In view of this fact, it needs to be said that "the oral tradition," *as it is invoked by these writers*, is an "invented tradition." It can be seen, as John Tomlinson has remarked, "as a phenomenon of modernity. There is a sense in which simply recognizing a practice as 'traditional' marks it off from the routine practices of proper [*sic*] traditional societies" (91). This is not, of course, to deny that there were and continue to be a number of oral traditions that "really" existed and continue to exist among the indigenous cultures of the Americas. Nor is it to deny that some contemporary Native American writers have considerable experience of "real" forms of oral performance. I am simply noting that "the oral tradition" as usually

---

9. Recall, however, that although an indigenous language was the first spoken language of these artists, English was their first written language.

10. Vizenor tends to claim ironies for the oral tradition as well, but this is a projection backward of present concerns. Primary orality must minimize irony for the simple reason that it is inimical to direct comprehension and ready recall.

invoked in these contexts is a kind of catchall phrase whose function is broadly to name the source of the difference between the English of Native writers and that of Euramerican writers. This "tradition" is not based on historically and culturally specific instances.

A quick glance at some of the blurbs on the covers or book jackets of work by contemporary Indian writers makes this readily apparent. When these blurbs are written by non-Indians (and most are, for obvious reasons, written by non-Indians), reference to "the oral tradition" usually represents a loose and vague way of expressing nostalgia for some aboriginal authenticity or wisdom, a golden age of wholeness and harmony. When these blurbs are written by Native Americans—this generalization I venture more tentatively—they are (to recall the discussion I offered in the first chapter of this book) a rhetorical device, a strategic invocation of what David Murray has called the discourse of Indianness, a discourse that has currency in both the economic and the political sense in the United States. Once more, to say this is in no way to deny that the narrative modalities and practices of a range of Native oral literatures, as well as the worldviews of various Native cultures, *are* important to many of the texts constituting a contemporary Native American literature, and not merely honorifically, sentimentally, or rhetorically.

Anyone who would make the claim that a particular Native text in English should be read as an instance of cultural translation must offer a specific demonstration of *how* that text incorporates alternate strategies, indigenous perspectives, or language usages that, literally or figuratively, make its "English" on the page a translation in which traces of the "foreign tongue," the "Indian," can be discerned. If one then wants to claim that this translation is indeed an anti-imperial translation, it becomes necessary to show how those traces operate in tension with or in a manner resistant to an English in the interest of colonialism.[11]

In the rest of this chapter, I will try to show how Leslie Marmon Silko's recent novel *Almanac of the Dead* (1991) is a powerful work of anti-imperial translation. Consistent with the methodology I have outlined, I must first point to a dimension of the novel that derives more nearly from an "Indian" than a Euramerican "language." I must then show that the ideological

---

11. It needs to be said that the very fact of difference, whether in form or in content, need not always and automatically work in the interest of resistance. See, in this regard, Fredric Jameson's 1988 account of "the social functionality of culture" (195–96), in which he notes that in spite of the fact that modernist and postmodernist art were both equivalently perceived as obnoxious, the former does in fact function in a manner that is oppositional to the cultural dominant, whereas the second has itself become the cultural dominant.

work this "Indian language" figuratively performs is one of resistance to imperialism.

Before doing so, as a context in which to place *Almanac*, I want to open up the question of the ideological work performed by contemporary Native American fiction in general over the past twenty-five years or so, a period that overlaps at least the more recent "postcolonial" period in the rest of the world. The account I give here should also be useful as a backdrop against which to consider Gerald Vizenor's 1991 novel, *The Heirs of Columbus*, the subject of my next chapter.

I will be going rather far afield for a theoretical framework to analyze the ideological work of some contemporary Native American novels—to Africa and to Kwame Anthony Appiah's account of the postcolonial African novel. I find Appiah's account highly suggestive for the topic of my concern.

Appiah describes the postcolonial African novel as falling into two fairly distinct stages; however, I will place contemporary Native American novels along a continuum—an adjustment I think Appiah would accept. In its first stage, according to Appiah, postcolonial fiction in Africa conceives of itself as specifically "anticolonial and nationalist." These novels of the late 1950s and early 1960s are "theorized as the imaginative re-creation of a common cultural past that is crafted into a shared tradition by the writer. . . . The novels of this first stage are thus realist legitimations of nationalism: they authorize a 'return to traditions' " (149–50). The authors of these novels, trained in Europe and America for the most part, are dependent on the African university, "an institution whose intellectual life is overwhelmingly constituted as Western, and also upon the Euro-American publisher and reader" (149). "In the West," Appiah notes, these authors are known "through the Africa they offer," whereas "their compatriots know them both through the West they present to Africa and through an Africa they have invented for the world, for each other, and for Africa" (149). In Africa, Appiah contends, "from the later sixties on, these celebratory novels of the first stage become rarer" (150), and a much more critical, "postrealist" or apparently postmodernist novel, the sort of novel exemplified by Yambo Ouologuem's *Le Devoir de violence* (1968)—in English, *Bound to Violence* (1968)—began to be produced.

Le Devoir de violence begins with what Appiah calls "a sick joke at the unwary reader's expense against nativism," and Ouologuem's "postnativist" novel continues on to provide "a murderous antidote to a nostalgia for *Roots*" (151). Novels of this second stage, "far from being a celebration of the nation, . . . are novels of delegitimation: rejecting the Western *imperium* it is true, but also rejecting the nationalist project of the postcolonial national bourgeoisie" (152). I am not competent to judge the accuracy of this very general account of the postcolonial African novel of the past thirty years or so, or of the particular reading it offers of Ouologuem. But let us see what happens when we bring only this much to the Native American novel of roughly the same period.

The so-called Native American Renaissance, as we noted at the outset of this book, is supposed to have begun with N. Scott Momaday's 1969 Pulitzer Prize for his novel *House Made of Dawn* (1968). It is surely the case that this novel establishes if not a specifically postcolonial stage, at least a self-consciously *new* stage of Native American fiction.[12] Momaday's novel and Silko's *Ceremony* (published in 1977 and in many ways indebted to Momaday's book) seem to work in much the same way as did the first stage of postcolonial African fiction as described by Appiah.

House Made of Dawn opens with its protagonist, Abel, a troubled mixed-blood veteran of World War II, running at dawn, "alone and . . . hard at first, heavily, but then easily and well," in a gray and rainy valley, where "snow lay out upon the dunes" (7). So too does Abel run, once more at dawn, at the novel's conclusion, only now he runs "on the rise of the song, House made of pollen, house made of dawn. Qtsedaba" (191). The final word is from the oral storytelling tradition at Jemez Pueblo, or Walatowa, where Momaday spent much of his early life, and it echoes "Dypaloh," the first word of the novel and the traditional marker of the onset of Jemez oral storytelling. The phrase "House made of pollen, house made of dawn" is from the Navajo "night chant" and it precedes the final words of the chant proper—"In beauty it is finished"—in which is indicated the completion of the healing or cure that is the primary purpose of the ceremony. Abel has learned these words from an urban Navajo named Benally who has "sung" over him. Short of a further discussion of this rich and complex text,[13] let

---

12. The interesting fiction of earlier Native American writers—writers like John Joseph Matthews, Pauline Johnson, John Milton Oskison, and D'Arcy McNickle, for example—has only recently begun to receive careful critical attention, and it remains to be seen whether a case can be made for considering *them* as the first generation of "postcolonial" or, indeed, anticolonial Native writers. For the present, however, there are good reasons to begin with Momaday.

13. Momaday's work has probably received more critical attention than that of any other Native American writer. Matthias Schubnell's book-length overview of Momaday's work is more hagiography than critical study, and a book-length study of *House Made of Dawn* has been published by Susan Scarberry-Garcia. Louis Owens's chapter on Momaday in *Other*

it suffice to say that *House Made of Dawn* appears to "authorize" at least the attempt to "return to tradition," legitimating a tribalism, nationalism (the two are largely synonymous in the Native American context although in opposition to one another in the African context), or conception of "Indianness" that it invents or constructs in more or less realist fashion "for the world" and also for Native Americans. Like the producers of Appiah's first-stage postcolonial African novel, Momaday has also been dependent on the American university (his much-noted Stanford doctorate with Yvor Winters, for example) and the metropolitan publisher (his book appeared under the imprint of Harper and Row)—and to remark this, I hope it will be clear, in no way denigrates Momaday's very substantial achievement.

Silko's *Ceremony* also appeared through a major eastern trade house, Viking, and Silko's early work was also supported academically.[14] Silko's protagonist, Tayo, is also a mixed-blood World War II veteran severely in need of healing. The novel chronicles Tayo's adventures in which he successfully lives out the vision "seen" for him by a somewhat odd but decidedly powerful Navajo shaman named Betonie. (Betonie's similarities to and differences from Momaday's Benally have been much discussed.)[15] Tayo successfully concludes his "quest" with a return to his people.[16] He is "cured," and the novel ends with a quasi-ceremonial invocation: "Sunrise, / accept this offering, / Sunrise" (275). The commitment to a "common cultural past," a "shared tradition," and a "return to traditions" is thus worked out in a structure that is circular and reintegrative, a comic structure, relative to a "real" world. Indeed, it is the ideologically functional point of the novel to insist that certain persons (e.g., Ts'eh Montano and her husband, The Hunter) and events (e.g., the appearance of the mountain lion) that might seem to be "mythic" are not mythic but "real." You can go home again, Silko's novel insists, for the traditional world of the Pueblos is available still.

If *House Made of Dawn* and *Ceremony* may thus be said to demon-

---

Destinies offers what I believe is the best overall account available. A. Lavonne Brown Ruoff's volume for the MLA gives most of the important references through 1990.

14. Silko was a student of Tony Hillerman's at the University of New Mexico and for eighteen months was a correspondent of the poet and teacher James Wright, whom she met at a writers' conference. For this latter association, see Silko and Wright, *The Delicacy and Strength of Lace.*

15. Ruoff is once more useful for references to the major criticism of Silko. See also the recent volume edited by Melody Graulich, "Yellow Woman."

16. My reference here is to Shamoon Zamir's extraordinary essay "Literature in a 'National Sacrifice Area': Leslie Silko's *Ceremony.*"

strate a very distinct "nostalgia for *Roots*," in Appiah's phrase, it seems
to me that this nostalgia is fully expressed in Momaday's long-awaited
second novel, *The Ancient Child* (1989), in which a middle-aged painter
named Locke Setman, or Set, with the help of a rather embarrassingly fan-
tasized nineteen-year-old woman called Grey, not only leaves his life in the
American metropolis but finds that his "true" or "authentic" identity was
always-already given in his name, Set, which means "Bear" in Kiowa. Set
increasingly "becomes" or discovers the bear in himself, learning that he
is a type of "the ancient child," the central figure in a Kiowa story about
a boy who became a bear. The novel reaches its climactic moment in the
light of a full moon as Set, "an awful quiet . . . in his heart," sees "the image
of a great bear, rearing. . . . It was the vision he had sought" (312). Here
too, an ideology of legitimation is expressed in an esthetic "eternal return"
consistent with the epigraph Momaday has chosen from Jorge Luis Borges
(it might also, of course, have come from Northrop Frye): "myth is at the
beginning of literature, and also at its end."

For all of this, it is still the case that even *The Ancient Child*'s commitment to the identities of myth cannot entirely ignore the differences of
history. If in little else, at least in Grey's (rather trying) fascination with the
legend of Billy the Kid and her citations of Shakespeare, James Joyce, Lewis
Carroll, and Wallace Stevens, Momaday makes clear his awareness that
even a young woman who is finding her identity as a traditional medicine
person can do so only in relation to the present-day world and its most
notable authors. Momaday had, of course, earlier indicated such an awareness in his portrayal of Benally, deeply attached to Navajo traditionalism yet
very much subject to the influences, usually deleterious, of the Euramerican world. And in *Ceremony*, Silko presents Betonie too as someone fully
cognizant of the fact that changes were necessary to "keep . . . the ceremonies strong" (133), as someone quite clear that the only way for tradition
to sustain itself is for it constantly to change. For all of that, in the three
novels I have so inadequately discussed, it does seem to be the case that,
like the postcolonial African novels of Appiah's first stage, what is offered is
"the imaginative re-creation of a common cultural past that is crafted into
a shared tradition by the writer" (Appiah 149–50), an ideological image of
Indianness for Native Americans and for the rest of the world. These novels present themselves in an essentially realist mode of representation (as I
have said, to insist on the "reality" of the "mythic" is part of the ideological
function of these novels) and in more or less comic, reintegrative structures.

Here the complicating instance of James Welch's work must be taken
into account. In what follows, I do not claim to offer full readings of the

texts I discuss but only to speculate on their ideological work in relation to the issues raised by Appiah. Welch's first novel, *Winter in the Blood*, appeared in 1974, after *House Made of Dawn*, therefore, and before *Ceremony*, and was published by Harper and Row (his subsequent novels have all been with New York trade presses: Harper, Viking, and Norton). His second novel, *The Death of Jim Loney* (1979), followed close on the publication of *Ceremony*. Although Louis Owens has titled his fine chapter on Welch "James Welch's Acts of Recovery" and has written of *Winter in the Blood* as achieving for its unnamed protagonist "a renewed sense of identity as Indian, as specifically Blackfoot" (*Other Destinies* 131), I read that novel as a bit more tentative in its conclusion—and indeed Owens himself later admitted, "The ending isn't exactly happy" (*Other Destinies* 146). And about *The Death of Jim Loney*, Owens quotes Welch himself: "The guy is going to kill himself. No, that's not funny" (*Other Destinies* 145).

Set, Tayo, and somewhat more tentatively, Abel resolve their problems by accepting an "Indian" identity of one sort or another. But this resolution is impossible for Jim Loney. Early in the novel, in response to his lover's rather silly exclamation—"You're so lucky to have two sets of ancestors . . . you can be Indian one day and white the next"—Loney thinks: "It would be nice to think that, but it would be nicer to be one or the other all the time . . . Indian or white. Whichever, it would be nicer than being a half-breed" (14). Later, the narrator, noting that Loney "never felt Indian," has him recall his lover's remark—"She had said he was lucky to have two sets of ancestors"—only to conclude, "In truth he had none" (102). Loney dies violently and alone.

Thus, ideologically, Welch's early fiction seems to fall somewhere between Appiah's first and second stages (hence my preference, at the outset, for conceptualizing these matters along a continuum). It is largely "postnativist"—postnationalist or posttribalist—yet mostly realist (even though *Winter in the Blood* certainly contains scenes that have, not inaccurately, been considered surreal). Nor does it have the sort of corrosive quality that marks Ouologuem's novel or, as we shall see, Leslie Silko's *Almanac of the Dead*. Welch's third novel, *Fools Crow* (1986), explores the Blackfoot past, which it treats as past. To say this puts me once more at a slight tangent to Louis Owens, who wrote of *Fools Crow*, "By imagining, or re-membering the traditional Blackfoot world, Welch attempts to recover the center—to revitalize the 'myths of identity and authenticity'—and thus reclaim the possibility of a coherent identity for himself and all contemporary Blackfoot people, that which was denied Jim Loney" (*Other Destinies* 157). If this is indeed the case, then Welch, by 1986, would have come to a position not far distant from that of Momaday or the Silko of *Ceremony*, authorizing at least a reclamation of, if not a return to, tradition. As I see it, however, Welch, in *Fools Crow*, presents the Blackfoot past as indeed past; the question, then, is whether (and *how*) this past might be a "usable past." Should this be the case, then Welch in some measure has departed from Momaday and the early Silko, coming nearer to those recent novels by Native American authors to which I will presently attend.

My argument thus far is that for all Momaday's and Silko's recognition of the need for tradition to change, in *House Made of Dawn*, *Ceremony*, and *The Ancient Child* these writers nonetheless insist on the possibility of a recuperation of the traditional—where, to be sure, the exact nature of the "traditional" remains to be specified. Nonetheless, to live in a "traditional" manner, within an organic "Indian" community, is presented as a tentative possibility for Abel and as an imminent reality for Tayo and Set. This is not the case, as I have said, for the protagonists in the first two novels of James Welch.

Neither able to "return to tradition" like Tayo and Set nor wholly cut off from it like Jim Loney—perhaps, then, somewhere between the Native American equivalent of Appiah's first- and second-stage postcolonial novel—are the protagonists in some recent fiction by Louis Owens, W. S. Penn, Diane Glancy, and Betty Louise Bell. Before proceeding, however, perhaps I should again say, as clearly as possible, what I am and am not attempting to do. I am *not* attempting to offer even a partial "survey" of contemporary Native American fiction; to do that would require attention to work by Sherman Alexie, A. L. Carr, Gordon Henry, Adrian Louis, Susan Power, and of course, Michael Dorris and Louise Erdrich, among many others. And I am *not* attempting to establish a canon of contemporary Native American writers, implying that the writers I choose to discuss are somehow the "best." Obviously I think these are very good writers, but their particular interest to me here concerns their relation to varieties of postcolonial ideological work. Demonstrating that relation is what I *am* attempting to do.

In Louis Owens's *The Sharpest Sight* (1992) we have the portrayal of two traditional Choctaw elders, Luther Cole and Onatima, or Old Lady Blue Wood. These two, although they have powers that can shift the compass and change the weather, are nonetheless sophisticated citizens of the modern world; they are college graduates given to meditating on the stories of *Moby Dick* and *Huckleberry Finn* and to critiquing published histories of their Choctaw people. They offer a sense of "home" to Cole McCurtain, Luther's nephew, and to Cole's father, Hoey. Indeed, the last words of the novel state, "In four days they were at the river, where an old man and old woman were waiting to take them home" (263). But the "home" these elders can offer does not seem to include the promise of reintegration into the sort of traditional community that Silko imagined for Tayo. Owens's meditation on tradition, moreover, is very much a meditation on tradition*s*, inasmuch as the novel concerns not only the relation between Cole and his powerful uncle but also the relation between Mundo Morales, a Mexican American, and his grandfather—who, having died sometime before the story takes place, appears only as a ghost. Near the end of the novel, the grandfather says: "My grandson has become more comfortable with the dead. . . . He knows at last who he is" (262). This suggests that Mundo has also, in some manner, come "home," but I think we will have to look to Owens's further work for a fuller sense of just where and what "home" is.

In Owens's most recent novel, *Bone Game* (1994), Cole McCurtain once more appears, and he is a professor at Santa Cruz, a social location and an identity quite unimaginable, I think, for Tayo or Abel and just exactly the sort of worldly placement that Set abandoned. To help Professor McCurtain through a very difficult time, Luther, Onatima, and Hoey all show up in Santa Cruz, where Cole's daughter, Abby, also has come. At the novel's end, Onatima and Luther return home to Mississippi, where they will talk to the bones of their Choctaw people and "tell them of their granddaughter in these strange, lightning-struck mountains" (242). Hoey by this time "has also found his world there," in Mississippi, and as Onatima says, "When the time comes he will surpass all of us" (242). (And he will surely be the subject of another further novel!) But for Cole, "home" just now is New Mexico and the house where he and his ex-wife were once happy, where they raised their daughter and where Cole wrote his books. He will take back to New Mexico a reinforced sense of the power of the Choctaw part of his background, but there is no question of a return to traditional community.

W. S. Penn's novel *The Absence of Angels* (1994) offers another portrait of a traditional yet entirely modern person, the narrator's grandfather, whose significant appearances at the beginning and end of the narrative provide a circular frame for the novel. Grandfather appears on the first page of the book, having just made the trip from Chosposi Mesa to Los Angeles—a fifteen-hour drive that "concentration" permitted him to make in eleven hours (in a 1947 Plymouth!). He has come to the hospital where Death hovers at the bedside of his newborn grandson, the sickly Albert Hummingbird, or Alley, the narrator and protagonist of the novel. Grandfather takes Death by the wrist, puts him in the passenger seat of the Plymouth, and drives him away—and Alley lives.

Grandfather not only drives a car but also pedals a bicycle—this too with great concentration—from which he falls, breaking a hip. Death, which had formerly and again recently stalked Alley, now appears at Grandfather's bedside, and the novel, like so many Native American novels, comes full circle in its last scene. Now it is Alley who visits his dying grandfather in the hospital. But Alley knows he cannot, indeed should not, try to drive death away, and Grandfather dies at exactly 10:21 P.M. on Christmas Eve, an hour and thirty-nine minutes short of the time he had predicted for his passing. Alley, with his lover, Sara Baites, scatters Grandfather's ashes across the desert, thinking about death and life and love and, finally, the life-sustaining value of laughter. Here too, although the power of a traditional person is celebrated, there still can be no return to tradition or to the consolations of "myth."

In Diane Glancy's 1993 collection of stories, *Firesticks*, six of the nineteen stories, each of which is called "Firesticks," form a linked series. *Firesticks* explores the relationship between a forty-two-year-old, part-Cherokee diner waitress named Turle Heppner and a drifter, a "dude" slightly younger than she (but also one-eighth Cherokee, "about a toe's worth" [28], maybe) known only as Navorn. When we meet them, Turle's father, William Bear Hall, is ill and dying, and Navorn agrees to drive Turle to see him in Frederick, Oklahoma, about three hours southwest of Guthrie, where Turle lives and works. Turle's father survives until the penultimate section of the series, when a call comes in to the diner telling Turle of his death.

In the meantime, Turle and Navorn have become lovers and then separated, although Turle now persuades Navorn one more time to drive her to Frederick to make funeral arrangements. Turle's father had asked to be buried on Mount Scott, in the Wichita Mountain range, "state property [and] solid granite" (55), as Turle notes in an explanation of why she has told her father that he could not accede to his wish. Turle says that when she looks at her father, she sees her grandmother's face. "He reminds me of the way she used to look. The few times I saw her" (38). Turle and her grandmother never spoke; "she didn't say anything" (40). Nonetheless, Turle explains: "She still speaks to me in a voice I can hear. It's as though what she had to say to me passed between us without speaking" (40). This silent communication is troubling to Turle, who has been "struggling for a language that would separate us. If I could have heard her, we would have parted like the people after Babel. I might not have liked, nor understood what she said. I would have had a chance to reject it. But we are together in our one language of silence. If she could speak, we could have separated"

(40). Even though her mother raised her, Turle, as noted above, sees her grandmother in her father's face, and "it's his family [she] feels on windy days when the dust is up." She adds, "In the red sumac groves I see the circle of their council fires." (41).

These "fires" are not literally those of her father's family, or not recently at any rate; the pronoun "their" seems to extend to people much further back, in a time when Cherokee council fires were struck by "firesticks." Among several visions and "memories" of things she cannot account for as part of her own historical experience, there is Turle's "dream," opening the final section of *Firesticks*, of "the burning firesticks the men used to carry from the holy Keetowah fire to light the smaller fires in the cabins." Turle notes: "It had been a yearly celebration. Light out of darkness. New life from the ashes. I dreamed of the firesticks passed from generation to generation. But now we had lost our ceremonies" (125). Yet Turle comes to understand that words are not only for separation and ending but also for joining and continuation. "Maybe," she says, "words are not always separators. If I speak light I have light. My words are firesticks" (126).

Navorn drives her to Mount Scott, "Holy ground" (129), as her father had called it, where Turle will bury his pipe and belt buckle. After doing so, she

> felt all people again. Those who lived long lives on the prairie, and those who knew extinction of their way of life. . . .
> The boulders on Mount Scott kept those faces before [her], frozen in fear and hopelessness. A band of Indians, massacred, their blood mingled with the red Oklahoma soil. (130)

Turle discovers that even if the ceremonies have been lost, there was "a place to go" after all. "The Spirit World kept all things that left. In my vision, the prairie moved again with herds of buffalo and antelope and Indian tribes. My father rode with them, their land restored" (131). *Firesticks* works to an ending in which Turle prays: "Comfort us, Great Spirit. And William Bear Hall, my other father, I'm sorry I did not bury you on Mount Scott like you asked" (131–32). In response, she hears, " 'Forgive me.' The answer was his this time" (132). The story concludes: "I see our words are firesticks finding a way through the dark. Strange warriors. In dreams I hear your talk" (132). The placement of "Strange warriors" as a free-standing fragment is curious. Had there been a comma rather than a period after "dark," "warriors" would have referred to words-as-firesticks. But that is not what the text gives us. Who, then, are these warriors? No doubt they are the Cherokees of old—word-warriors (to use a phrase that has been associated with Gerald Vizenor), carriers of the firesticks of the old council fires. In some measure memories, most particularly dreams and visions, bring them back.[17] But to "have" them, to make them "real" and make them stay, requires words: "our words are firesticks" (132).

Those last words are Turle's words, and words for her are spoken (or unspoken), heard, remembered, and dreamed. But they are not written; Glancy is the writer of words, and *Firesticks* may certainly be taken in part as an affirmation of the author's sense of her vocation. As Silko does in *Storyteller*, Glancy in *Firesticks* presents herself, by implication, as one who writes words "for the people." Turle Heppner can be heard because Glancy gives her the words—words like those of Turle's earlier vision in which she saw "antelope running and . . . saw buffalo, herds and herds of buffalo, as they once had been on the prairie. . . . Just as someone some-day might get a vision of what our lives had been. They came back not to haunt nor accuse but to remind that they once had been, *and still moved with the swirling winds on the plains and the clouds across the sky*" (93, my emphasis). Turle will go back to work in the diner in Guthrie; she and Navorn will or will not stay together. Outwardly at least, her life will probably not look so very different from the lives of the non-Native inhabitants of her hometown. But the story has made clear that for her, what "once had been" "still moved." The ceremonies are gone, and one cannot reconstitute and live the traditional past. But that past has a presence as well, one that may have powerful effects.

Like Owens's fiction, Betty Louise Bell's 1994 novel, *Faces in the Moon*, offers a traditionalist couple, and like Glancy's fiction, it shows a move to memory and language as important in the maintenance of tradition. Here, Great-aunt Lizzie and Uncle Jerry are people who provide a center and

---

17. The role of memory in all of the novels I have discussed so far, and in Betty Louise Bell's *Faces in the Moon*, which I discuss below, is important. Rather than attempt to examine memory as some sort of unique and autonomous expression of Native American culture and value "in its own right," we might find a more fruitful exercise in comparing it with its role, say, in Proust, Woolf, Faulkner, and even Eliot, among other of the canonical modernists. As Boas showed long ago, to assert a "comparative method" as a measurement of *value* (e.g., higher or more "civilized" compared with lower and more "primitive") is to produce inac-curacies, absurdities, or indeed abominations—just what those Native critics committed to cultural or intellectual "sovereignty" and "autonomy" have tried to circumvent. But there are other sorts of comparison available, and to ignore them is unnecessarily to foreclose pos-sibilities for understanding. Because I have been misunderstood on this point before, I need to add explicitly that I am *not* suggesting that one should bring the assumptions one brings to Proust to these novels, but rather that one should see whether one can find a critical lan-guage that might mediate between Proust and Native American fiction—yet again, as this chapter takes it up, an issue of cross-cultural translation or ethnocriticism.

give a sense of "home" to Lucie, the child the narrator once was. But there is no nostalgia here for "roots." Lucie will not return to the old ways or go "home" again with any prospect of permanence. So far as the novel offers, in Appiah's words again, "a common cultural past . . . a shared tradition," it is a tradition that cannot be discovered in a "return" of any kind but rather remains to be (re-)produced—as with Glancy—in language. But Lucie is not Turle Heppner; she not only will speak but also will become, as she announces on the penultimate page of the novel, the arrogant whiteman's "worst nightmare: . . . an Indian with a pen" (192), more specifically, an Indian *woman* with a pen.

The novel begins powerfully with the following words: "I was raised on the voices of women. Indian women." These voices are sited at "the kitchen table . . . a place of remembering, a place where women came and drew their lives from each other" (4). The novel ends with "the advice" the narrator says was "passed on to [her] by the old people" (193). And what is this "traditional" wisdom passed on by the old ones? It is: "Don't mess with Indian women. . . . That's all. You don't need to know more than that." These words, spoken by the narrator, are echoed by the ghostly voices of other women: " 'Don't mess with Indian women,' the voices whoop" (193). There is imagined here not so much a return to tradition and community as, instead, the necessity of writing, of producing tradition and community, specifically the community of Indian women who today may draw their lives from each other not only at the kitchen table but in a wider world beyond.

Bell's novel—like the work of Owens, of Penn, of Welch, and of Glancy and even like the Native American novels paralleling Appiah's first-stage postcolonial African novel—is written in a sophisticated mode of realism (i.e., a realism *after* modernism). Its form—in this it is like some but unlike others of the novels I have mentioned—contrapuntally plays a circular structure of return (back to the old ones, to kitchen-table talk) against a linear structure of "progress" (forward to self-discovery and writing). The book is a female *kunstlerroman*—a portrait of the artist as a young woman—charting the narrator's progress as an outward (in William Bevis's terms, a centrifugal)[18] movement into the world. But this movement outward depends on a centripetal structure of return, one that, as I have said, takes place in memory or imagination.

Let's return to the final scene of the novel, which I have only partly de-

18. See Bevis, "Native American Novels."

scribed above. It is set in the Oklahoma Historical Society, where Lucie has come to "look at the Cherokee rolls" (190) and fill in the lacunae of her past. Here is an image of the Foucauldian archive, constitutive of what may be known, thought, or spoken or of Virginia Woolf's library of the British Museum, where women exist only insofar as men have pronounced on them. It is in response to "the librarian's" contemptuous grin and his question "Who do you think you are?" (191) that Lucie allows her anger to erupt and then to voice the tough-minded wisdom of the old ones. But her cry, "Don't mess with Indian women," even as it is echoed by ghostly voices, does not conclude the novel. Rather, the book ends with a sentence that on first reading I thought anticlimactic but that I now see as necessary. After the "whoop" of the voices repeating the refrain "Don't mess with Indian women," the narrator says, "And I hear Auney say, slow and pleased, 'Naw, I sure wouldn't wanna do that' " (193).

Lucie's Aunt Auney, her "mother's chorus since birth" (10) and the survivor of four marriages with difficult men, appeared on the first pages of the novel as an image of a strong woman; yet "the closest she came to fighting back was to refuse to forget" (11). Nor will Lucie forget, but she will also most definitely fight back, with her voice and her pen. So again there is a movement out, of "progress" or advance, but as well a movement back, a return in memory to the kitchen table as home. But this return will not ideologically authorize anything like the presumed satisfaction, unity, or plenitude of a precolonial past.

Here I will return at last to Leslie Marmon Silko's *Almanac of the Dead* (1991), a book that is very different from *Ceremony* and that has distinct affinities with Appiah's second-stage postcolonial African novel. In *Almanac* there is no pueblo to which one may return, no kiva in which one may feel related to the gods, the ancestors, and the earth. It is almost as if Silko had taken the celebrated advice given to Marlow in Joseph Conrad's *Lord Jim*: "In the destructive element immerse." For this novel, unlike *Ceremony*, is not set in the mid-1940s but in the horrific present, where drug deals, the pornography of torture, traffic in weapons and body parts, and elaborate and cynical real estate scams define the Western "culture of death" in the Americas.[19] I will try to describe a single strategy of this

---

19. The phrase "the culture of death" comes up frequently in Silko's work, as it does as well in the work of Gerald Vizenor, to which I will turn shortly. In his encyclical letter of March 30, 1995, titled *Evangelium Vitae*, or *Gospel of Life*, Pope John Paul II used the term "culture of death" to name a secular humanism that is, in the pope's view, indifferent to "the original inalienable right to life" (*New York Times*, March 31, 1995). Although the pope and

novel that seems to me to come, figuratively speaking, from a "language" other than "English," a strategy that is deployed in decidedly anticolonial fashion, so that *Almanac*, in the ways I have indicated above, may be read as an example of anti-imperial "translation."

Almanac devotes 763 pages to illustrating the statements Silko has placed in two boxes in the lower left-hand and lower right-hand corners of an annotated "Five Hundred Year Map" of northern Mexico and the southwestern United States; the map is printed just after the table of contents (of the paperback edition). The left-hand box, labeled the "Prophecy" reads: "When Europeans arrived [in the Americas], the Maya, Azteca, and Inca cultures had already built great cities and vast networks of roads. Ancient prophecies foretold the arrival of Europeans in the Americas. The ancient prophecies also foretell the disappearance of all things European." The right-hand box, called "The Indian Connection," states: "Sixty million Native Americans died between 1500 and 1600. The defiance and resistance to things European continue unabated. The Indian Wars have never ended in the Americas. Native Americans acknowledge no borders; they seek nothing less than the return of all tribal lands."

    Almanac imagines a contemporary continuation of "The Indian Wars," telling of the movement of apocalyptic armies from north to south and from south to north to rid the Americas of "all"—or at least a great many—"things European." Not all of Silko's Indian warriors are of Native American ancestry, and her cultural politics is not racialized. Thus, from the north, New Age pop spiritualists, guerrilla eco-warriors, homeless Vietnam War veterans, Lakota militants, a barefoot Hopi, and a Korean-American computer genius, among others based in the United States, begin a march southward, while a "People's Army" of Indians from Central America, led by nonviolent twin brothers and a Mayan woman who believes in hand-held missile launchers and rockets, marches northward through Mexico. Both groups will eventually converge on Tucson, the eccentric center of the story, and the meeting of these two forces, still to come at the novel's end, will signal the beginning of the end of the dominance in the Americas of the settler culture.

    The specific strategy of resistance I want to describe in *Almanac of the Dead* is its insistence on a north-south/south-north directionality as central

---

certain Native American writers are in agreement in their condemnation of what they variously consider the Western "culture of death," I do not think they would necessarily agree as to what constitutes a life-giving culture.

to the narrative of "our America" (in the phrase of Fernández Retamar).[20] This shift in the directionality of history in itself works as an ideological subversion of the hegemonic Euramerican narrative, whose geographical imperative presumes an irresistible ("destined") movement from east to west.

As Roy Harvey Pearce claimed more than forty years ago, "The history of American civilization would . . . be conceived of as three-dimensional, progressing from past to present, from east to west, from lower to higher" (49). The image of east-west movement, like other "images of centrality," in Edward Said's phrase, gives "rise to semi-official narratives with the capacity to authorize and embody certain sequences of cause and effect, while at the same time preventing the emergence of counternarratives" (1988, 58). East-west images found a "semi-official" narrative of American progress, of the fulfilment of a "manifest destiny," that will take this nation "from sea to shining sea." But "facing west," as Richard Drinnon's powerful study of that name shows, also founds "The Metaphysics of Indian-Hating and Empire-Building." Perhaps I can best convey the depth and persistence of east-west images in the construction of American imperial dominance by citing the words of that great empire builder (and Nobel Peace Prize winner!) Henry Kissinger, who, sometime in the 1980s, said: "You come here speaking of Latin America, but this is not important. Nothing important can come from the South. . . . The axis of history starts in Moscow, goes to Bonn, crosses over to Washington, and then goes to Tokyo. What happens in the South is of no importance" (in Clausen 634). In the hegemonic narrative of the dominant culture, the movement of history is always from east to west, and that movement can neither be reversed (to go from west to east would be the same as going from higher to lower, from civilized to savage, something unthinkable) nor be adjusted to accommodate the south, where, as Kissinger insists, "what happens . . . is of no importance."[21]

---

20. Silko's map does have a single horizontal line indicating the movement of several of the characters eastward, from San Diego to Tucson, and others westward, from El Paso to Tucson. The north-south/south-north directionality seems, however, of central importance.

21. Cf. Dirlik, "The Postcolonial Aura":

> It may not be fortuitous that the North-South distinction has gradually taken over from the earlier division of the globe into three worlds, unless we remember that the references of North and South are not merely to concrete geographic locations but are also metaphorical. North connotes the pathways of transnational capital, and South, the marginalized populations of the world, regardless of their location. (351)

But it is exactly this inexorable east-west narrative that Silko contests. Insisting that history happens north to south, south to north, she shifts the axis of *where* is important, thus shifting the axis of *what* is important. The novel concludes with the return to Laguna Pueblo (where Silko grew up) of a "giant stone snake" that had disappeared. The novel's last sentence reads, "The snake was looking south, in the direction from which the twin brothers and the people would come" (763). This "looking south" rather than "facing west" is not only a change of geographical perspective but also a metaphor for a change of cultural and political value. In terms elaborated by Gerald Vizenor, Euramerican "dominance" is, here, challenged by Native American "survivance," the former committed to progress, the latter to "continuance."[22]

Silko's "armies," as I have said, are composed of a ragtag collection of people—African American, Asian American, Euramerican, Native American. Will these poor inherit the earth? If the novel has gone well, we should hope so, whoever we are, and identify with *them*. To say this permits me a return to Yambo Ouologuem's novel *Le Devoir de violence*, in regard to which Appiah wrote, "If we are to identify with anyone, *in fine*, it is with " 'la négraille'—the niggertrash, who have no nationality" (152). As Appiah reads Ouologuem, however, this potential identification with "la négraille" is not a happy one. For them, for those "who have no nationality," "one republic," Appiah states, "is as good—which is to say as bad—as any other." In this stage of the African novel, "postcoloniality has become . . . a condition of pessimism," "a kind of *post*optimism" (155). Yet Ouologuem's "postrealist" "delegitimation" of "nationality" and of "the postcolonial national bourgeoisie" is not strictly consistent with the "postmodernist" project according to Appiah, because it is "grounded in an appeal to an ethical universal . . . a certain simple respect for human suffering" (155). This "ethical universal" Appiah unashamedly names "humanism," noting the way in which this makes the apparently postmodernist, postcolonial African novel "not an ally for Western postmodernism but an agonist from which . . . [Western] postmodernism may have something to learn" (155). I would say much the same for the apparently postmodernist Native Ameri-

---

As we shall see, in similar yet also very different ways, Silko's North and South are also both "concrete" and "metaphorical."

22. I'm not sure just where Vizenor first began to develop his concept of "survivance," although most recently it appears fictionally in his *Heirs of Columbus* (1991) and essayistically in his *Manifest Manners* (1994). What is necessary for survivance is healing, something important to Silko. I examine Vizenor's commitment to healing in the next chapter.

can novel.[23] For it too, as Appiah wrote, what "role postmodernism might play . . . is . . . too early to tell" (157).

The choice to respect human suffering and to reject nationalism is, as Appiah reads Ouologuem, a choice of "Africa—the continent and its people" (152), and we may take this observation back to Silko's text. *Almanac*, like the postcolonialist African fiction of Appiah's second stage, is certainly an instance of "postrealist writing," offering a "postnativist politics . . . [and] a *transnational* rather than a national solidarity" (155), but it is not, for all the grimness of its detail, pessimistic.

Let me take these two matters one at a time. First, my sense of *Almanac*'s commitment to "a *transnational* rather than a national solidarity" once more puts me at odds with Elizabeth Cook-Lynn, who claims that the book "insists upon the nationalist's approach to historical events" in its creation of "a Panindian journey toward retribution." But Cook-Lynn's very next sentence admits: "[*Almanac*] fails in this nationalistic trend since it does not take into account the specific kind of tribal/nation status of the original inhabitants of this continent. There is no apparatus for the tribally specific treaty-status paradigm to be realized either in the Silko fiction or in the Pan-Indian approach to history" (*Cosmopolitanism, Nationalism* 34). But surely this is to recognize that *Almanac* is not so much failing in its nationalist approach as simply not taking such an approach at all. *Almanac* not only is committed to Pan-Indianism rather than tribal nationalism—as Cook-Lynn herself realizes—but also is committed to a kind of Pan-Americanism, in which all those who adhere to tribal values of life and healing may join, regardless of blood quanta or enrollment cards. I will return to these matters below and will take them up again in the next chapter in regard to what I will call Gerald Vizenor's *ratio*-nalist rather than *natio*-nalist approach, an approach that is nearer Silko's than Cook-Lynn's.

As for *Almanac*'s "optimism," perhaps this may derive from the fact that Silko, like other contemporary Native American writers, lives in a postcolonial world but writes, as I have said, from within a colonial context. Materially, that is, sociopolitically, things are not good, but there is everything yet to be done to rid the Americas of bad European things

---

23. I will, in fact, be saying exactly this in regard to Gerald Vizenor's *Heirs of Columbus* in the next chapter. I here only repeat that the contemporary Native American novel, although it may perform ideological work that parallels the postcolonial novel in Africa or elsewhere, remains, as a consequence of its sociopolitical situation, a colonial production in a postcolonial world.

and values. Of course the world of drug deals, body parts sales, and violent pornography that Silko describes is horrible to contemplate, but it is
premature for "*post*optimism." What Cook-Lynn called "retribution" Annette Jaimes refers to as the dispensation of "a long overdue measure of
justice to the haughty current minions of [the] malignant Euroamerican
order."[24] This, Jaimes notes, "is what ultimately makes the novel . . . a
work of life and liberation rather than death and despair" (57). *Almanac*
insists that the prophecies are not to be mocked; the Americas *will* return
to the values of life. These are, to be sure, the old values of indigenous
tribal peoples, but they are, today, to be represented by a "transnational"
"négraille"; whatever it might mean to speak of a choice of "Africa—the
continent and its people," Silko's "armies" are an image of "America—the
contentinent(s) and its people" today: a transnational "tribe" committed
to healing, to continuance and survivance. These values are also important
to Gerald Vizenor, and it is to Vizenor's work that we turn next.

---

24. Justice, for Jaimes, will be dispensed by "the dispossessed/disenfranchised indigenous vanguard swarming northward" ("Review" 57). But there is, as I have noted, a movement
southward toward justice and life-giving values as well.

3

Ratio- *and* Natio-
in Gerald Vizenor's
Heirs of Columbus

GERALD VIZENOR'S *THE HEIRS OF COLUMBUS*, WITH ITS PUBLICATION IN 1991 positioning it as a sort of preemptive strike against the anticipated excesses of the Columbian quincentenary, seemed most immediately to present itself as a Native American reappropriation of the "Admiral of the Ocean Sea," a postmodern or postcolonial recolonization of the Columbian legacy. The novel's comic reinvention of Columbus for our time is, to be sure, important; yet the *Heirs of Columbus,* as its title should have— although in 1991 it probably could not have—made clear, is as much about the *heirs* of Columbus as it is about the old sailor for Spain.

The nature of heritage—the principle according to which members of a group might define their identity and relationship—had been an important concern of Vizenor's for some time. The novel preceding *The Heirs of Columbus*—*The Trickster of Liberty*, published in 1988—was subtitled *Tribal Heirs to a Wild Baronage*, and in 1990 Vizenor's first novel, *Darkness in Saint Louis Bearheart* (1978), was reissued under the new title *Bearheart: The Heirship Chronicles.* In 1991 *The Heirs of Columbus* moved heirship, again as a principle of collective identity and coherence, to titular and thematically controlling status. In what follows, I will read *The Heirs of Columbus* as an intervention in the age-old battle between *natio* (the Latin verb means "to be born" and carries with it all the filiative and racial claims of birth, descent, and blood inheritance) and *ratio* (the verb means to "rea-

son" and carries the affiliative, cultural, and consensual claims of chosen
values). In his Columbus book, as I hope to show, Vizenor takes what might
seem a very surprising position on the importance of *natio-*, one that would
seem at odds with the values or ideology of the community consolidated at
the end of the novel: the posttribal utopian community devoted to healing.[1]

Even a short history of the relations between *natio-* and *ratio-* in the West
would take us far afield and take me well beyond my competencies. But
a few things do need to be said. By the time of Columbus, as Marc Shell
has written, the "Statutes of the Purity of the Blood (*limpieza de sangre*)
adopted in Toledo in 1449—and elsewhere a little earlier or later . . . made
the distinction between Christian and *converso* [Jewish convert] solely on
the basis of blood *lineage*" (309–10, my emphasis).[2] The Spain that expelled its Jews in 1492 (and its Moors ten years later) rejected the notion
of identifying with those of Jewish heritage through any relation of con-
sanguineous kinship. It rejected, that is, the logic of those who argued that
we are all (blood) brothers in Adam or, for that matter, the logic of those
who made the point that, after all, Christ was a Jew. But it rejected as well
the logic of a relationship with Jews based on spiritual kinship, denying—
irrationally, it would seem—that a Jewish convert was if not a brother in
blood at least a brother in Christ. By 1492, as Shell continues, "the myth
of Pure Blood (*sangre pura*) unmixed with Muslim or Jewish blood" (311)
had taken hold, and so the Jews were expelled. Columbus, in his log for
the day he set sail, remarks on the heavy traffic in the harbor caused by the
many ships bearing Spain's Jews away.

The various types of traditional "blood" reasonings—only my directly
traceable blood kin are my brothers, and those who are my brothers must
be my directly traceable blood kin—were to be left behind by a modern or "enlightened" worldview in which one identifies one's brothers and

---

1. *Bearheart* and *The Trickster of Liberty* also conclude with the establishment of posttribal utopian communities of healing. The survivors of the western pilgrimage in *Bearheart*
came to rest at Pueblo Bonito, in Chaco Canyon, New Mexico, where they encountered
three tribal holy men who "laughed and laughed knowing the power of their voices had restored good humor to the suffering tribes" (243). *The Trickster of Liberty* does not end with
the laughter of the sages but with the barking of mongrels ("the mongrels barked on the
meadow" [154]), a very positive presence and a very salutary sound in Vizenor's work, as
we shall see. My use of *posttribal* is an analogue of Vizenor's delineation of what he calls the
"postindian," most particularly in his *Manifest Manners*.

2. A *converso* is a Jew who has more or less voluntarily chosen to become a Christian, as
opposed to a *marrano*, a Jew who has accepted forced conversion, for example, under torture
or threat of death. *Marrano* means "pig." *The Heirs* speaks of both *conversos* and *marranos*.

sisters as *citoyens* and *citoyennes*, eventually comrades, or indeed "my fellow Americans." In the modern world of the *Aufklärung*, not *natio-* but *ratio-* was to be the basis for identifying one's kin: my brothers and sisters are those who share my values and principles. From this perspective, all *natio-*nalisms—appeals to birth and blood as the basis of kinship and heirship—appear to be, in the phrase of Tony Judt, "pathological condition[s] of incomplete 'modernity' " (44).[3] Nonetheless, we know it to be the case that nationalism today is both obsolete and powerful. Thus, for a progressive politics of invention, modernist *or* postmodernist, it would seem necessary to reject the logic of *natio-* in all its forms. With only this brief background, let us turn back to Vizenor's *Heirs of Columbus*.

Who was Columbus, and who are his heirs? What serves to identify and relate them? On the first page of the novel, Columbus is said to be "an obscure crossblood who bore the tribal signature of survivance" (3). Columbus is a "crossblood" in that—and this is one of the novel's central conceits—"Columbus was Mayan" (8) and also Jewish on his mother's side. According to Stone Columbus, one of the heirs of Columbus and the protagonist-figure in the novel,[4] it was "the Maya [who] brought civilization to the savages of the Old World" (9).[5] Columbus's achievement was to bring "tribal genes back to the New World"; his was no voyage of discovery but rather a return "to his homeland" (9). The Mayas are important to Vizenor's ethnomythology in that they "were the first to imagine the universe and to write about their stories in the blood" (26). The phrase "stories in the blood" occurs approximately fifty-three times in a novel of 189 pages and is one to which I will return.

Not only was Columbus Mayan but so too, we are informed, was Jesus Christ—who, like Columbus, also had a Jewish mother and was, thus, himself a cross-blood. In Vizenor's account Jews, particularly Sephardic Jews

---

3. Native tribalists, nationalists, or traditionalists, however, see modernity as the pathological condition; for them, the rationalist or scientific view of the world is a misreading of what is best apprehended sacrally. But not all traditionalists, I believe, would require actual blood relationship as a marker of kinship.

4. I am thinking of Donald Barthelme's novel of 1967, *Snow White*, in which various characters are—with witty, postmodern irony—the prince *figure*, the wicked witch *figure*, and so on. Vizenor would no more create a traditional protagonist than Barthelme would offer a straight analogue of the characters in the fairy tale.

5. Carter Revard's brilliant satire "Report to the Nation: Claiming Europe" may well have provided a partial source for this notion. Revard's essay chronicles his travels from England to Greece, where, at strategic points along the way, Revard speaks words and makes gestures that "claim" these yet-barbaric territories for the Osage nation.

like the Mayans, "bear their stories in the blood" (101). Not only Mayans and Jews but also Moors (although to a somewhat lesser degree) are important to the novel. For the Moors' "ancient leaders were crossbloods" as well, and Moorish people also "bear the signature of survivance and remember stories" (34). This "signature," alluded to many times in the novel, is a specifically genetic signature, and Stone Columbus can legitimately claim to be an heir of Columbus because he has "naturally" inherited "the same signature" as Columbus, as "confirmed in several reliable studies of his bones and dried blood on a lead ball found at the bottom of his casket" (135).[6]

It is Stone Columbus who leads the heirs, along with a motley crew of— to take a phrase from Vizenor's *Bearheart*—"weirds and sensitives" (35 and passim), in the founding of a posttribal utopian community at Point Assinika (Point Roberts in the Strait of Georgia between Washington State and Vancouver Island, Canada).[7]

On October 12, 1992, exactly five hundred years after Columbus's first day in the New World (but a bit after this novel appeared), a "sovereign nation" dedicated to healing is founded.[8] In a parody of a well-known passage of Columbus's journal, the narrator says that "at dawn," the heirs "saw pale naked people, and . . . went ashore in the ship's boat" to take "possession of this point in the name of [their] genes and the wild tricksters of liberties" (119).[9] Thus is established "the first nation in the histories of the modern world dedicated to protean humor and the genes that would heal" (189). So the healing that is to take place in this "natural nation" (126) is to be achieved both by the humor in stories and by advanced genetic therapies— *ratio-* and *natio-* in tandem, it would seem, as these are conjoined in the key phrase to which I have already alluded, "stories in the blood."

---

6. Barry Laga's recent study of *The Heirs* expends a good deal of ingenious energy relating Derrida on the "signature" to Vizenor's use of that term. I think, unfortunately, that this is wasted ingenuity inasmuch as whatever "signature" *might* mean in Vizenor's text, it is clearly used to mean genetic signature exclusively.

7. The citizens of this new nation are a heterogeneous and, indeed, rather strange lot. I will speak of them a bit more below. The nation is watched over or represented by (either way will do) the statue called The "Trickster of Liberty," at the base of which the remains of Pocahontas are buried next to the remains of Christopher Columbus.

8. October events are particularly prominent in *The Heirs.* Not only Columbus's first landing but also Vizenor's birthday is in October.

9. An odor of sanctity for these proceedings is provided by the fact that the heirs make "all the necessary declarations and [have] these testimonies recorded by a blond anthropologist" (119). The mockery of anthropology is an ongoing theme in Vizenor's work.

Still, I admit to having found this a troubling locution. This is because I do not believe that there is any gene for narrative orientation or preference or that stories can be inherited "naturally," remembered, listened to, or heard "in the blood." Michael Elliott cites Vizenor's *Manifest Manners*: "Native American identities are created in stories . . . memories, visions, and the shadows of heard stories are the paramount verities of a tribal presence" (56). But, as Elliott notes, this move, intended to free Indian identity questions of what Vizenor calls "the manifest manners of dominance"— enrollment cards, blood quantums, and the like—has its own problems, for Vizenor never does say *which* stories, memories, or visions are to count as indicators of tribalism. In *The Heirs of Columbus*, that problem is ostensibly addressed by specifying *healing* stories as among the "paramount verities," but there the matter is confused by assigning those stories to the "blood."

Now it is certainly true that some genetic inheritances are advantageous for survival under specific ecological conditions, but that is not the issue here.[10] What is centrally at issue, as we shall see further, is the commitment "to heal rather than steal tribal cultures" (162), a *ratio*-nalist not a *natio*-nalist commitment. Nonetheless, when Stone Columbus very early in the novel announces that "the truth is in our genes" (10), what is one to think?[11]

As if to forestall worries of this sort, the narrator announces that the phrase "stories in the blood" is a "*metaphor* for racial memories, or the idea that we inherit the structures of language and genetic memories" (136, my emphasis). But these phrases are simply variants of one another; "stories in the blood" is in synonymous, not metaphorical or figurative, relation to the notion of "racial memories." What, then, are we to make of this apparent embrace of the logic of *natio*-, of race and blood, in a writer all of whose work has been militantly antiracist?

For what the narrator says of Stone Columbus might very well be said of Vizenor himself.[12] He "resists the notion of blood quantums, racial identification, and tribal enrollment. The heir is a crossblood, to be sure, but

---

10. That is, the issue in general is not dealt with in a consistent manner. For example, Columbus is said to have possessed "an enormous clubbed penis curved to the right, a disease of fibrous contracture during an erection" (31), the source not of pleasure but of great trouble and pain. But if this genetic legacy has been passed on to Stone or others of the heirs, "in the blood," it is not mentioned.

11. The only rejoinder to Stone's remark is Luckie White's rapid and rather bemused, "Right, we are what our genes must pretend" (10). To my mind—a mind anachronistically committed to making *sense*—this works only in translation: "Right, whatever we are, we pretend comes from our genes." But that is not what Vizenor has written.

12. This is not to suggest that Stone is an alter ego of Vizenor or that parts of the novel

there is more to his position than mere envy of unbroken tribal blood. Indians, he said, are 'forever divided by the racist arithmetic measures of tribal blood.' He would accept anyone who wanted to be tribal, 'no blood attached or scratched' " (162). Stone's intention in founding the nation at Point Assinika is "to make the world tribal, a universal identity, and return to other values as measures of human worth, such as the dedication to heal rather than steal tribal cultures" (162). Yet Stone himself, as we have noted, is an heir of Columbus not only because of his values and his dedication to healing but also because of his genes, or "blood."

Chaine Louis Riel, himself the heir of a famous métis rebel, reports of the community at Point Assinika, "Their scientists have established the genetic signatures of most of the tribes in the country" (162). And now, "anyone could, with an injection of suitable genetic material, prove beyond a doubt a genetic tribal identity. Germans, at last, could be genetic Sioux, and thousands of coastal blondes bored with being white could become shadow tribes of Hopi, or Chippewa" (162).[13] This commitment to the *genetic* possibility of "a universal tribe would cause no harm, 'because there was nothing to lose but racial distance' " (162). Thus it seems unequivocally clear, as I have noted, that any racialist argument in *The Heirs of Columbus* is set squarely against racism. But why, then, does *The Heirs* embrace *natio-* as equal to or even more important than *ratio-* in the conceptualization of heritage and community? Does not this at least apparently give aid and comfort to the forces that Vizenor's work has always sought to resist?

I think the answer has to do with Vizenor's self-conscious, indeed, militant adoption of a postmodern strategy marked, in Linda Hutcheon's phrase, by "a deliberate refusal to resolve contradictions" (*Poetics* x).[14] This entails the consequence that whereas postmodernism "is certainly political," as Hutcheon affirms, it must be "politically ambivalent, doubly encoded as both complicity and critique" (*Politics* 168). It is the apparent embrace of *natio-*, or blood reasoning, I shall argue, that is the complicitous

---

should be read autobiographically. I consider the conditions of possibility for that sort of reading of Vizenor's work in the next chapter.

13. So even this "genetic tribal identity" will be a *mixed*-blood identity, for example, German Sioux, coastal blonde Hopi, and so on.

14. In interview after interview, from early in his career until just recently (e.g., see Miller, "Mythic Rage and Laughter: An Interview with Gerald Vizenor" [1995]), Vizenor has insisted on his own "refusal to resolve contradictions" as a deliberate device in the interest of a freedom defined as the infinite multiplication of possibilities. For all of that, as I discuss below, it is not a technique or an ideology consistent with the definition of freedom as adherence to specific liberatory arrangements, that is, to the establishment of healing communities.

part of a critique that is carried by a commitment to *ratio-*, the reasoned decision to accept into the community any who have chosen to heal rather than steal.

I should make clear that in reading *The Heirs* in this fashion, I am in no way claiming to specify Vizenor's intentions or to be engaged in uncovering what he "really" means to say. In trying to figure out how the unironic use of a phrase like "stories in the blood" might not be politically retrograde—as N. Scott Momaday's use of such phrases, whatever his intention, tends to be—I am somewhat in the position of the talk-radio host and Sephardic Jew Luckie White. That is, just as she is "impatient for conclusions," so too am I as a reader; both of us are, for good or ill, in possession of "a worldview that was frustrated by the heirs who imagine the starts but never the ends" (173). Vizenor has imagined all the starts and has quite self-consciously refused to imagine the "ends," leaving things, in currently approved fashion, "open."

Thus, so far as I am concerned to imagine possible ends, I am inevitably working against the grain, attempting not so much to resolve the contradictions that Vizenor has refused to resolve as to examine the likely ideological implications of that refusal. This will undoubtedly be taken by some as seeking to impose "closure," a sin synonymous with the imposition of colonial monologism or some such—as though one could read the ideological tendency of texts from their formal gestures alone, as though one could automatically take certain (newly) conventional signifiers of "openness" (paradoxicality, refusal to resolve contradictions, etc.) as "good" (anticolonial, egalitarian, etc.) independent of context. When I say such things as Vizenor does this or that, I am not, let me repeat, presuming to know his intentions, to "speak for" him, or to claim superior wisdom; rather, I am attempting to say what the text itself does not, will not, or cannot say and to offer an estimate of the worldy directionality—the ideology—of both textual assertions and textual silences.

To pursue this matter for just another moment, let me say that this is no more than what literary criticism, in one form or another, has done since its emergence in post-Socratic Greece. If one wants to reject the useful application of such a procedure to Native American or any other "other" literature because it is Western, and thus imperialistic, that is fine. But what, then, is one to put in its place? As I have argued in the first chapter, there is no purely indigenous, autonomous, "Native" mode of criticism for written texts, for reasons that are obvious. One might, of course, engage in the traditional critical practice available to the oral storyteller and offer a retelling of a story in such a way that the differences from any prior telling constitute "critical" commentary. In some measure this is what Aimé

Césaire has done in rewriting Shakespeare's *The Tempest* and what Chinua Achebe has done in rewriting Joseph Conrad's *Heart of Darkness*. But even these rewritings are in Europhone languages and take the grounds of their critique from the imperial originals. They are inevitably intercultural acts or, in my own term, *ethnocriticism*.

Without for a moment forgetting or denying the importance to Vizenor of his personal (but also textual) experience of Anishinaabe culture—his interest in the trickster-creator Manabozho, in the terrible man-eating windigo, in bone and shell games—we also have to remember the importance to him of Japanese and Chinese culture and, of course, of French postmodernisms. What is true of Vizenor is true for Leslie Marmon Silko (e.g., as noted above, her apprenticeship with Tony Hillerman, her correspondence with James Wright, her appreciative reading of Henry James) and for the majority of contemporary Native American writers (cf. Louis Owens's play with William Carlos Williams, T. S. Eliot, Robert Frost, and other American poets). In view of the intercultural formation of these writers' texts, *only* an intercultural criticism, some variant of an ethnocriticism, has any hope of providing insight. "In order for criticism to be responsible," Talal Asad has written, "it must always be addressed to someone who can contest it" (156). But, as noted in chapter 1, what is most usefully contested is the form and content of the critical statement, not its presumptive origins in a particular culture or identity. To attempt to articulate the silences of a text and its discursive effects in metanarrative fashion is simply to practice *criticism*—and criticism of this sort is Western, to be sure. But saying this in no way denies criticism's value for the comprehension of contemporary Native American literature. Let me here return to my reading.

So far as Vizenor does keep things open by refusing to resolve contradictions, then the politics of his novel must remain ambivalent. So far as he chooses to adhere to certain gestures of postmodernism, then his "fantastic historiography," "Fabulation," "mythomania," or "outright tall tales"—these terms are all from Fredric Jameson (368)—must be, on the one hand, as Jameson has written of postmodern fiction generally, symptoms "of social and historical impotence, of the blocking of possibilities that leaves little option but the imaginary" (369), all these things being consistent with Hutcheon's complicitous side of the coin. But on the other hand, as Jameson points out, postmodernist fiction may also "by its very invention and inventiveness endorse . . . a creative freedom with respect to events it cannot control," thereby stepping "out of the historical record itself into the process of devising it." Postmodern fantastic historiography, thus, may proliferate "new multiple or alternate strings of events," which, as Jameson continues, "can rattle the bars of the national tradition and the history manuals whose very constraints and necessities their parodic force indicts. Narrative invention here thus becomes the figure of a larger possibility of praxis" (369). Everything Vizenor has ever written means to ally his work to the "figure of a larger possibility of praxis," and these words of Jameson's accord well with Vizenor's claims for the postmodern imaginary fabulations in which he has for so long engaged—claims consistent with the critical dimension of his project.[15]

As I read *The Heirs*, then, the complicitous side of Vizenor's project is the acceptance without criticism (without, that is, the usual undercutting irony) of a logic of *natio-*, a logic oriented, however, toward the critical effect of upholding a logic of *ratio-*. Thus, throughout the book there is an acquiescence to—in Herbert Marcuse's old phrase—"the real as rational," which today would seem to mean the real as national. Because it is the case that not secular reason but blood ties are in ascendance everywhere, if birth, blood, and race seem the only secure basis of heirship, then let us complicitly (at least seem to) assent to the fact that, in Marc Shell's phrase, "blood *counts*" (310n).

Stone Columbus can, then, unqualifiedly affirm that the "truth is in our genes" (10) and go on to found a universal tribal community in which all will share a blood lineage, a certain genetic "signature." But because genetic signatures need no longer be inherited, it is possible to provide them on the basis of *ratio-*, not strictly *natio-*; at Point Assinika, those who get to share tribal blood are only those who share tribal values. All who are committed to healing by means of the humor in stories can now literally be brothers and sisters "in the blood." Since blood does count—as it seems to, for all the rationalists' efforts to the contrary—then let it count, and let all those who would heal and be healed come to the Dorado Genome Pavilion at Point Assinika, where the values they have freely chosen can be inscribed in their "blood" by means of a generous genetic technology.[16]

---

15. For my understanding of Hutcheon and Jameson on the postmodern novel, I am grateful to Brian McHale's "Postmodernism; or, The Anxiety of Master Narratives." Complicitous critique is, as McHale underlines, a fairly unstable oxymoronic construction, and as McHale further notes, in Jameson's analyses of specific texts it is unclear on what basis he determines that there is more complicity than critique and vice versa. Hutcheon is much too wary of appearing to choose one side or another—that would be so *un*postmodernist—to attempt this kind of sorting out.

16. In addition to the Dorado Genome Pavilion, in which genetic research in the interest of healing takes place, the second major institutional edifice at the new nation is the Felipa Flowers Casino. Gambling and the workings of chance are of some importance in

The democratic distribution of what we might call "designer genes" is specifically intended to lead to racial mixing and what the Ku Klux Klan used to call (still does?) the "mongrelization of the race." For Vizenor, this is all to the good, for the mixed-blood, cross-blood, or "mongrel" is the exemplary type for a postcolonial, postmodern, post-Indian world. As Caliban, "the great white reservation mongrel" (16), explains, it was mongrels who

> dreamed humans into being and then out to sea in search of their
> own stories in the blood, but humans lost their humor over land,
> gold, slaves and time. Mongrels created the best humans, we had that
> crossblood wild bounce in our blood. (16)

It is the "crossblood wild bounce" of the mongrel that the novel celebrates, insisting that "the best humans" are mongrels: Columbus, Jesus, Mayans, Jews, Moors, and those who will come to Point Assinika for a genetic transfusion. Though blood may count in *The Heirs of Columbus*, "good" blood is not the mythical *sangre pura* privileged by racists of every stripe but is always-already mixed blood. As Sergeant Alex/Alexina Hobraiser put it in Vizenor's *Trickster of Liberty*, "Mixedbloods are the best tricksters, the choice ticks on the tribal bloodline" (xii).[17]

Tricksters, like mongrels, have long been important to Vizenor, who has invoked and created them again and again in his work. Short of a full discussion, it may suffice to note here that tricksters, for Vizenor, are (whatever else they are or are not) mythic comedians, and the "protean humor of tricksters"—indeed, humor in general—as Chaine Louis Riel states, "has political significance" (166). Vizenor has always viewed his humor as having "political significance," but as I have remarked in relation to Hutcheon and Jameson, so far as he allies himself to postmodernism, any political significance he can achieve must be an ambivalent political significance, complicitous and critical at once. Nonetheless, in *The Heirs of Columbus*,

---

The Heirs, as in other of Vizenor's texts. Louis Owens usefully notes that Vizenor's commitment to chance, even though it celebrates openness and possibility, nonetheless denies "our responsibility for ordering and sustaining the world we inhabit," a responsibility "that is central to Native American ecosystemic cultures" (*Other Destinies*, 234). Owens admirably tries to resolve this contradiction by reference to Vizenor's tricksterism, citing Paul Radin's classic (and also contested) definition of the trickster as one who "knows neither good nor evil yet is *responsible for both*" (*Other Destinies*, 239, my emphasis). Whatever this may have meant in relation to premodern, sacral Native American cultures, it can hardly mean the same thing in the modern, "posttribal" context that Vizenor invokes. This is a variant of the "refusal to resolve contradictions" issue.

17. Alex/Alexina obviously raises questions of (possible confusions of) gender identity, a subject that occurs again and again in Vizenor's work. A good study of this matter is needed.

Vizenor's concluding image of children dancing, safe (for the moment at least)[18] within the protective confines of a community of healing, is an image of something far less ambivalent and far more stable than postmodern fiction typically permits itself. Vizenor concludes the novel proper with a "structure of feeling" (in Raymond Williams's sense) of what Appiah calls "left modernism," as though it were possible, for example, to have your Baudrillard and Jean-Paul Sartre too.

For it is indeed Sartre who sets the tone for our reading of the book; it is Sartre whom Vizenor has chosen to provide a lengthy epigraph for *The Heirs*. (And, I should note, it is a single epigraph; this is very different from most of Vizenor's texts, which have three or four or more epigraphic quotations.) The text Vizenor has chosen comes from Sartre's *What Is Literature?* In Bernard Frechtman's translation, it begins with a variation on Marx's famous shift in philosophical purpose. Sartre wrote, "We are no longer with those who want to possess the world, but with those who want to change it." For all his recognition that "the most beautiful book in the world will not save a child from pain," nonetheless Sartre insists, "We want the work to be . . . an act; we want it to be explicitly conceived as a weapon in the struggle that men wage against evil."

As we have remarked, the posttribal utopian community established at Point Assinika is centrally concerned with healing children, with saving them from pain; Stone Columbus's "ambitious course" in founding the nation looks forward to the rescue of "millions of lonesome and wounded children" (122). It is at the Dorado Genome Pavilion, under the direction of Pir Cantrip (accused by nefarious figures of being a former Nazi but, in fact, a "wounded Jew" and one of the good guys), that genetic research in the interest of healing is carried out; and children arrive from all over to be saved from pain.[19]

---

18. My parenthesis refers to the fact that there is always a "moccassin game with demons" (183), a gamble with the destructive windigo, again and again to be engaged. As noted above, games of chance have consistently been important to Vizenor's work. I comment briefly on one particular such game, a dish game or *passagewin*, in the next chapter.

19. In the Felipa Flowers Casino, behind the bingo tables, "at the back near the restaurant and concessions," is located the "Parthenos Manicure Salon" (138). Here, those like Teets Melanos, along with Harmonia Dewikwe, "hear the secrets of women and the concessions [*sic*] of men, more than a shaman or a priest would hear on the reservation" (141), and, by their loving attention to the hands of their clients, perform important acts of healing. But they also save "thousands of secret bits of skin and fingernail from the hands" (141) of those they manicure—in the interest, of course, of the positive genetic research being carried on at the Dorado Genome Pavilion. Traditionally, however, the saving of bits of skin and nails is an activity performed not by those with benevolent intentions but rather, by witches who

If this is Vizenor's version of the Sartrean aspiration, where can it come from? Sartre's sense of cultural politics, to say what is obvious, bases itself on distinctions between "authenticity" and "inauthenticity," "good faith" and "bad faith," indeed on the determinable difference between social "good" and "evil." But these distinctions and differences are only an illusion from the antifoundationalist perspective of the Baudrillardian, DeLeuze, and Guattarian postmodernism with which Vizenor has again and again linked his practice; they are closures of the sort Vizenor has always abhorred.

For all of that, *The Heirs of Columbus* commits itself in quite unambiguous and unironic fashion to the vision, as I have said, of a posttribal community dedicated to healing, a community that will save children from pain. The last sentence of the novel reads (there is, however, an epilogue), "The children danced on the marina, and their wounds were healed once more in a moccasin game with demons"(183). Such a conclusion cannot come from postmodernist proliferations of relativism or ironic celebrations of irresolution. So, once more, where does it come from? Again it seems to me that it comes from what I have earlier quoted Appiah as calling a "certain simple respect for human suffering," that same "humanist" recourse to an "ethical universal" that I remarked animates Silko's *Almanac of the Dead*.

In Vizenor's novel too, the community with which we are to identify is a rag-tag, mongrel community of cross-bloods, not much different from those who make up Silko's revolutionary armies or Ouologuem's transnational "négraille." Community members include, for example (I have mentioned her above), Admiral Luckie White, host of a talk show on Carp Radio and, as it turns out, a Sephardic Jew. There is Harmonia Dewikwe, a "government manicurist" (118), co-worker with Teets Melanos at the back of the Felipa Flowers Casino in the Parthenos Manicure Salon. There is, importantly, Pir Cantrip, the wounded Jew, survivor of the Holocaust, in charge of genetic research at the Dorado Genome Pavilion. Sir Pellegrine Treves, also a Sephardic Jew and an expatriate from London, joins the community as well. There is a child named Blue Ishi, and

---

mean harm. This traditional aspect of the novel, unlike others (e.g., reference to the windigoo, to mythical gambling, to medicine pouches, to miigis shells, and so on), seems one the reader is called on to ignore rather than to integrate into any reading.

Here, as elsewhere, the reader will not have missed the oddity of characters' names in Vizenor's work. In the following chapter I comment generally on Vizenor's ideas about the meaning of names and about naming practices. But a more specific study of names in Vizenor's work is needed.

there is the no-name transvestite, "a pale weaver with a doctorate in consciousness studies from the University of California" (118), who dresses
as "either Eleanor Roosevelt, Nancy Reagan, or, his favorite, Lady Bird
Johnson" (132).[20] Memphis, the panther, Caliban the great white mongrel,
and a good many others make up the posttribal society at Point Assinika.
These people (and animals), like Silko's armies from the north and from
the south, may also be read as the equivalents of Ouologuem's "négraille,"
those without nationality or, indeed, specific tribal affiliation.

Just as Appiah has noted how "Africa's postcolonial novelists . . . anx-
ious to escape neocolonialism are no longer committed to the nation" (353),
so too may we note that Vizenor is no longer committed to the "tribe."[21] As
though following Frantz Fanon's dictum that national independence is no
more than the immediate goal that, once achieved, must strive for the more
substantial goal of human liberation, Vizenor, like Appiah's postcolonial
novelists, is interested in the *universal* tribe, a category—inasmuch as it can
include Sephardic Jews, Germans, coastal blondes, and a host of others—
that is not merely "pan-Indian," not merely a choice of "Africa" (or
pan-Africa), not even here of "America," but again of suffering humanity.

So far as this is so, in the end (indeed, literally *at* the end of *The Heirs
of Columbus*) Vizenor, like Silko, like Ouologuem, may turn out to be
"misleadingly postmodern" (Appiah 353), or quite simply, it may be that
Vizenor's postmodernism can serve as an antagonist to Western postmodernism rather than an ally. In its sensitivity to a pervasive human suffering
and its desire to act, in the Sartrean manner, on behalf of that suffering, this
is a postmodernism that takes a position far less ambiguous than anything
possible in the more usual postmodernisms of Europe and America.

This is the ideological implication, as I see it, of Vizenor's practice, although I must once more acknowledge that he might not see or mean it that
way. Yes, Vizenor's commitment to what I have called a posttribal utopian

---

20. Vizenor taught for a while at the University of California–Santa Cruz, whose "History
of Consciousness Program" is doubtless the object of the satire. In *The Heirs of Columbus*,
as in almost all of his other fiction, there are numerous semi-private references and jokes. I
am referred to on pp. 110–11.

21. Yes, it is true that Stone Columbus will accept into the community "anyone who
wanted to be tribal" and "to heal rather than steal tribal cultures" (162). It is true as well
that in *Manifest Manners*, as elsewhere, Vizenor speaks approvingly of the "verities of a tribal
presence" (56). But in *Dead Voices*, which we shall examine shortly, Vizenor has the focal
character, Bagese Bear, sorrowfully admit, "The tribes are dead voices" (136). It seems fairly
clear that for Vizenor, post-Indian tribalism will not be so much a matter of particular national allegiances (e.g., the Lakota nation, the Navajo nation) based on blood kinship (or
enrollment cards) as a matter of tribal *values*. Here too is matter for further study.

community devoted to healing is quite unambiguous; it is not ironic. But, again, this commitment cannot logically be derived from anything that has preceded it. In a certain sense (what sense? logical? esthetic? moral? all of these? none of these?), because *The Heirs of Columbus* is a text that has exerted enormous amounts of energy and ingenuity to keeping everything open, refusing to resolve contradictions, the final sentence-image is entirely unearned and arbitrary. It *feels* heartfelt; it seems to work, but is that a deception rather than an achievement? Again, I cannot say—and all the while I am aware that my agonizing over not being able to say is easily dismissible by Vizenor as yet one more "tragic" "anthropological" error, an anachronism.

I have tried to offer a reading that can enlist *The Heirs of Columbus* as "a weapon in the struggle that men wage against evil," to see its enthusiasm for a revised concept of *natio-* as somehow consistent with a (post)Enlightenment adherence to *ratio-* or reasoned choices of values. As I have acknowledged on several occasions, this is my way of valuing Vizenor—even though I cannot justify "my way" by claiming that it is "really" his way. I read him further "my way" in the next chapter.

4

Dead Voices, *Living Voice: On the Autobiographical Writing of Gerald Vizenor*

DEAD VOICES, (1992) GERALD VIZENOR'S MOST RECENT NOVEL, IS ALSO, I believe, his most personal or autobiographical novel. Its protagonist, although not "really" the author, resembles him more nearly than the protagonists of any of Vizenor's other fictions; moreover, *Dead Voices* is a book centrally and explicitly concerned with the uses of stories for "survivance," a matter of considerable importance to Vizenor for some time. The origin or placement of stories—that is, whether they are "in the blood" or come from elsewhere—is not at issue here, as it was in *The Heirs of Columbus*; rather, the issue is whether stories can perform their healing function only as voiced or oral stories or whether they can retain their power—whether they can avoid simply becoming "dead voices"—when they are in written form. *Dead Voices* also takes up a number of other issues that Vizenor has addressed in his autobiographical or essayistic writing (the texts in which he speaks more or less in his "own" voice), such things, for example, as names and nicknames, pronouns, and the comparative political efficacy of the pen versus the sword or gun.

In this chapter I will be reading the "fictional" text *Dead Voices* as though it were in some measure "true." I will thus be blurring, far more than is inevitable, the generic line between the autobiography or personal essay and the novel, a line drawn on the Western epistemological distinction between "truth" and "fiction." I will mention some Western critical perspectives that might provide a rationale for such a reading, although it will be Native American perspectives on these matters from which I will draw my primary justification. The result should be an ethnocritical account of *Dead Voices*.

Just one word further: the fact that I situate *Dead Voices* in the context of Vizenor's autobiographical writing should not be seen as an attempt to peer into the psyche of its author. Although this does not strike me as an inherently disreputable practice, it is not a practice in which I am here engaged. As noted above, *Dead Voices* struck me as closer to Vizenor's autobiographical texts than to his novels, and thus I attempt to correlate these texts with *Dead Voices*.

Vizenor has published at least four autobiographical texts: "I Know What You Mean, Erdupps MacChurbbs: Autobiographical Myths and Metaphors," in 1976; the brief "self-portrait" (for Jane Katz's *This Song Remembers: Self-Portraits of Native Americans in the Arts*) titled "Gerald Vizenor, Ojibway/Chippewa Writer," in 1980; "Crows Written on the Poplars: Autocritical Autobiographies," in 1987; and the book-length *Interior Landscapes: Autobiographical Myths and Metaphors*, in 1990. I say "at least four," but this phrase could be replaced by "perhaps five or six or even more" if we include the abundantly self-referential essay "The Envoy to Haiku" and "The Tragic Wisdom of Salamanders," the latter with—as Vizenor himself notes—its "several autobiographical references" (personal communication), both published in 1993, or if we go back to 1984 and parts of Vizenor's *The People Named the Chippewa*. One could also say that Vizenor has published "only one" autobiography if we require autobiographies to be book-length texts (*Interior Landscapes*).

From a Western perspective, to read a novel as a type of autobiography, treating its protagonist as "really" or nearly speaking directly for its author, is to violate what Philippe Lejeune calls the "fictional pact"[1] and thus apparently to confuse (to say "blur" here begs the question) genres traditionally kept distinct. A naive violation of this sort might lead one, in effect, to offer sociology or psychology where "literary criticism" should be. A more sophisticated violation of the "fictional pact" might follow Lejeune a bit further, to the point where one might justify an autobiographical reading of a fictional text by claiming its affinity with the

---

1. This phrase should be read in conjunction with "the autobiographical pact," as I shall note further below. See Lejeune, "The Autobiographical Pact," and "The Autobiographical Pact (bis)."

curiously hybrid texts Lejeune calls "fictitious fiction[s]."[2] These include, on the one hand, Gertrude Stein's *The Autobiography of Alice B. Toklas* and, on the other, certain dialogues of Plato and Jean-Jacques Rousseau's *Rousseau juge de Jean-Jacques* (Rousseau judge of Jean-Jacques), texts that offer what Lejeune calls "fictitious witness."

Dead Voices might be made to fit this latter category by following Lejeune's observations (he is, in turn, following Emile Benveniste) on the deictic rather than strictly referential nature of pronouns in autobiographical writing.[3] And a fuller search of the expanding corpus of theoretical work on autobiography than I have attempted would, no doubt, provide other rationales for reading *Dead Voices* in relation to if not actually *as* autobiography. Let this serve, however inadequately, to provide a Western perspective on this matter.

But Gerald Vizenor is a Native American writer, so that we must also take into account indigenous views on these matters. Although we cannot hope to find traditional perspectives on such generic types as the novel or the autobiography, certainly there are Native views on narrative, the discursive modality we have already noted as centrally important to Indian peoples. What is curious to add is that many traditional Native narratives do not seem to divide along the lines of truth and fiction.

This is not to deny that Native Americans distinguish between stories they understand to be true and those they regard as false. The Plains peoples' customary practice that coup tales be told in the presence of people able to confirm or deny the veracity of the deeds being claimed is only one of several testimonies to their distinction between true and false. But, as Donald Bahr, an anthropologist whose work has been with the Akimel O'odham and Tohono O'odham (formerly Pima and Papago) peoples of the Arizona desert, wrote, "To my knowledge tribal societies do not have *fictions* in the modern sense of stories that people make up with no pretense or faith that the characters in the stories really lived or that the characters' actions really occurred" (47). Commenting on "Hohokam history" (the Hohokam were the ancestors of the Pima and Papago), Bahr has more recently noted, "All the stories or myths on this subject should be taken as good faith histories

---

2. See Lejeune, "Autobiography in the Third Person." The references in the sentences immediately following are from this essay, 31–52.

3. Cf. Ducrot and Todorov, *Encyclopedic Dictionary*: " 'Deictics' are expressions whose referent can only be determined with respect to the interlocutors. . . . Emile Benveniste has shown that . . . their very meaning . . . even though it depends on language, can only be defined by allusion to their *use*" (252, my emphasis).

. . . offered by their tellers as *true*" (7, my emphasis). Robert Brightman noted of the Rock Cree people that stories they call *ācaðōhkīwin*, stories of the ancient times, conventionally labeled "myth" by Westerners, "are generally said to be *true* accounts of events that transpired in an earlier condition of the world . . . the stories were relations of then contemporary events that were handed down successively through the generations" (7).

Here let me note in passing that the distinction between "history" and "myth," so important to the West, also seems to exist in Native cultures. But whereas the West bases its distinction between myth and history on a judgment of the fictionality or truthfulness of the narrative in question, indigenous peoples tend (I am unable to say whether this is a generalization that does indeed apply continent-wide, and I offer it for what heuristic use it may have) to make this distinction on the basis of the distance (earliness) or nearness (recentness) of the events narrated, very distant events having the aura of what we would call "myth" (though they are still "true") and more recent ones being responded to more nearly as history (also, but in no greater degree, "true").

Wendy Wickwire, who worked with Harry Robinson, a traditional Salishan storyteller of the Northwest (British Columbia), claims: "Harry never fictionalized stories. Indeed the very concept of fiction was foreign to him" (*Native Power* 20). This seems largely to be the case with what is known of other contemporary oral storytellers.

As it is for contemporary oral storytellers, so too may it be for at least some contemporary Native American writers. I offer, casually enough to be sure, an anecdote told by the linguist William Bright, who, as part of his work on an anthology that would be called *The Coyote Reader*, wrote to Peter Blue Cloud telling the poet of his interest in "the mythic Coyote." Blue Cloud sent back a postcard saying, "You sure Coyote is a myth?"(xix). In the same way, Clifford Trafzer, a mixed-blood Wyandot and former chair of the Department of Ethnic Studies at the University of California–Riverside, begins a recent essay called "Grandmother, Grandfather, and the First History of the Americas" with a quotation from the Okanogon writer Mourning Dove, who noted that stories about the Animal People "are not myths nor [*sic*] fiction; they are real history, true accounts of what happened near the Beginning when the World was very young" (474). In his essay, Trafzer generally supports Mourning Dove's view.[4]

---

4. For something more on the myth-history distinction, see my "American Histories, Native American Narratives."

Thus the stories that Native Americans listen to and tell can be taken as "true" (i.e., they "really" happened, they are not "fiction"), no matter how improbable they may appear from a realistic perspective (e.g., the intervention of supernaturals). These stories, whomever they may actually tell of—gods, monsters, animals—and whenever they may actually have happened, are considered to be functionally relevant to present situations, bearing directly on the lives of presently existing people. Indeed, as Julie Cruikshank points out, there are very definitely "behavioral models in narrative" (344), some stories specifically offering ways to engage in the "cultural constructions of individual experiences" (339). Let me assemble just a few illustrations of this point from contemporary Native American oral performance and from contemporary Native texts.

In an important paper of 1984, the anthropologist Keith Basso described in detail the discursive practice of what he calls "Stalking with Stories" among the western Apaches. These Apaches use the narrative category of *'agodzaahi*, or historical tales, "to criticize[,] to warn[,] or to 'shoot' " (36) people who have behaved in a manner inappropriate to the Apache way. Basso tells of a seventeen-year-old Apache woman, recently returned home from boarding school, who attended a girl's puberty ceremony "with her hair rolled up in a set of pink plastic curlers" (39) even though "Western Apache women of all ages are expected to appear at puberty ceremonials with their hair worn loose"(39). Not to do so is not only disrespectful but potentially threatening to the ceremony's "most basic objectives, which are to invest the pubescent girl with qualities necessary for life as an adult" (40). Two weeks later, this young woman was present at a family birthday celebration. As Basso tells it, after the meal was over, the woman's grandmother narrated a version of a traditional historical story, said to have occurred sometime in the latter nineteenth century, about a forgetful Apache policeman. Immediately the young woman stood up and left the gathering. She left because, as the grandmother explained to Basso, "I shot her with an arrow" (40). And, indeed, this young woman understood the story to be "stalking" her; she recognized that the communally-agreed-upon moral of the story was not to behave too much like the "whiteman."[5]

The story-arrow shot by the young woman's grandmother spoke literally of someone else, but as Basso notes, "every historical tale is also 'about' the person at whom it is directed" (39) and speaks directly to that person's behavior and sense of self. I emphasize Basso's account of the western

---

5. I use the spelling that Basso uses in another important text, *Portraits of the "Whiteman,"* an account of Apache humor making fun of Euramericans.

Apaches' practice of stalking or hunting with words because Vizenor has independently invented the term *wordarrows*,[6] and—a matter to which I will return—in his autobiographical writing he several times notes occasions on which he himself made the choice to hunt, or "stalk," with the pen rather than with the gun.

Cruikshank, to whom I have already referred, provides the fullest account of the way in which Native people—in particular, Native women—use traditional stories in the telling of their own lives. In her work with three Yukon Native elders—Angela Sidney, Kittie Smith, and Annie Ned—Cruikshank learned "how these women use traditional narrative to explain their life experiences" (2), how they combine "traditional narrative with individual experience to construct a coherent account" (xi) of their lives. Cruikshank adopts this "'bifocal' perspective" in the published text of Angela Sidney's life history by alternating chapters that "approximate a conventional Western understanding of life history and include events [Sidney] either experienced herself or heard about from older people" with "traditional narratives she also wanted to record as part of her life story" (29).

This is consistent with Melody Graulich's recent statement about Native Americans: "You claim who you are by the stories you accept as your own, the particular stories you tell and retell"(5). This would seem to be the case not only for contemporary Native oral storytellers but as well for many contemporary Native writers; Graulich's comment comes in an introduction to a book of critical essays on Leslie Marmon Silko. N. Scott Momaday, in *The Way to Rainy Mountain*, constructs his Kiowa identity, as is well-known, in part by retelling the traditional stories of the Kiowas. Silko herself, in *Ceremony*, wrote, "You don't have anything if you don't have the stories" (2). Her autobiography, mixing "fictional" and "factual" discourse, is called *Storyteller*. A very great many other writers might be mentioned here, but I will quote only some lines by Simon Ortiz from a poem called "Survival This Way":

> *We travelled this way,*
> *gauged our distance by stories*
> *and loved our children. . . .*
> *We told ourselves over and over*
> *again, "We shall survive*
> *this way."(168)*

---

6. See, for example, Vizenor's collection entitled *Wordarrows: Indians and Whites in the New Fur Trade*. An early essay (1986) by A. LaVonne Brown Ruoff is called "Woodland Word Warrior: An Introduction to the Works of Gerald Vizenor."

Here we find, made explicit in the work of a contemporary Native American writer, the linkage of storytelling to survival so important to traditional oral cultures. This linkage has been important also to Gerald Vizenor, and it is particularly important to him in *Dead Voices*, a story about stories that I shall read as "true" in the sense that its stories, although they are about someone else, also may speak of Vizenor himself. By telling these stories, Vizenor in important measure accepts them as his own, thus—as I quoted Graulich just above—claiming who he is.

Dead Voices begins in February 1982 and ends ten years later in February 1992. The first and last chapters are narrated by a lecturer at a California university, a man known only as "Laundry."[7] He has been given this nickname by the main character of the book, a Chippewa woman named Bagese Bear, from the Leech Lake Reservation in Minnesota. Bagese tells seven stories as she turns the cards of an Anishinaabe (Chippewa) card game call "wanaki."[8] Each of the cards pictures an animal, and according to Laundry, Bagese "explained that the players [of the wanaki game] must use the plural pronoun *we* to share in the stories and become the creatures on the cards" (17). Bagese's insistence on the plural pronoun is related to her insistence that "tribal stories must be told not recorded, told to listeners but not readers, . . . heard through the ear not the eye" (6). To Laundry's early assertion that "written words are pictures," she responds: "Printed books are the habits of dead voices. . . . The ear not the eye sees the stories." To his rejoinder that "the eye hears the stories," she insists, "The voices are dead" (18). Printed stories are nothing but "dead voices."

As the narrator informs us, Bagese actually turned into a bear about a year before the novel begins. It is to the absent Bagese that Laundry Boy addresses the final words in the book—"We must go on"—words that Bagese herself had several times pronounced. He offers these words in explanation of his decision to publish Bagese's wanaki stories despite his promise "not to publish what she told [him]" (6–7) and despite her warning that publication would kill the stories.

---

7. Vizenor is, of course, a professor at a California university, although I do not know of any nicknames for him.

8. Early in *Dead Voices*, the narrator speaks of the "wanaki chance," a "game of natural meditation, the stories that liberate shadows and the mind" (16), adding that "the word 'wanaki' means to live somewhere in peace, a chance at peace" (17). Much later Bagese says, "The wanaki game is our war with the wordies and the peace of their dead voices" (140). I have not found "wanaki" listed as an Anishinaabe game in any of the references I have examined.

My very brief synopsis has sought to foreground the importance to *Dead Voices* of the apparent conflict between the oral and the textual transmission of stories, noting an attention to names, nicknames, and pronouns. All of these have been concerns of Vizenor's for a long time. I will deal with the subject of "writing the oral tradition," in Kimberly Blaeser's phrase, at considerable length below (this will also provide a segue to the issue of pens and swords or guns), but I turn here to a discussion of Vizenor's interest in names, nicknames, and pronouns.

In 1984, Vizenor published a text called *The People Named the Chippewa*, meditating on what it means to know oneself as *anishinaabe* or *anishinabeg* (plural) but to be named—or, of course, misnamed—*Chippewa*. In a piece called "Native American Indian Identities: Autoinscriptions and the Cultures of Names" (1992), Vizenor continued his meditations on these matters, and in the recent *Manifest Manners* (1994), he speculates on how to name "Indians" in a "postindian" age, beginning the chapter "Ishi Obscura" with the words, "Ishi was never his real name" (126). (A few years ago, Vizenor also attempted to get the University of California at Berkeley to rename [Alfred] Kroeber Hall as Ishi Hall, an effort that so far has not met with success.) In 1985, he named Dennis Banks, of the American Indian Movement (AIM), "Dennis of Wounded Knee," then, in *The Trickster of Liberty* (1988), named him (the character in the novel may also refer to other Native politicos) Coke de Fountain. It appears likely that the author and media star Jamake Highwater appears in *The Trickster* as Homer Yellow Snow, and other examples of Vizenor's renamings of people might easily be added. Vizenor has also expended a great deal of imaginative energy on the names of the invented characters in his fiction: Inawa Biwide, Rosina Cedarfair, Griever DeHocus, Father Mother Browne, Belladonna Darwin-Winter Catcher, Transom Molte, and Justice Pardone Cozener, to mention only a very few. Examples of Vizenor's fascination with names and naming throughout his career could easily be multiplied; and I have already noted some of the curious names in *The Heirs of Columbus*.

Nicknames have also been of interest to Vizenor, who has engaged them from early to late in his work for what may be personal as well as political and esthetic reasons. His father, Clement Vizenor, horribly murdered before Vizenor was two, was known by the nickname Idee; his mother, who more than once abandoned him, was nicknamed Lovey (see *Interior Landscapes*). In *The People Named the Chippewa*, Vizenor approvingly notes Frances Densmore's attention to Chippewa nicknames (14), and in *Dead Voices*, the narrator learns the meaning of Bagese's name from her uncle, nicknamed Sucker; the name "means a tribal dish game in translation"

(143), from *pagessewin* (bû´gese˝win). Most recently, *Manifest Manners*, with reference to Matei Calinescu, nicknamed AIM activist Clyde Bellecourt "kitschyman" (154). Once more, many further examples could be listed.

In "The Ruins of Representation," in the new introduction to *Summer in the Spring*, and elsewhere, names and nicknames, Vizenor suggests, tell stories.[9] In *Summer in the Spring*, for example, he wrote: "The stories of nature were heard in names. Place names and personal nicknames were communal stories. The *Anishinaabe* were never alone in their names, visions, and stories" (10). Pronouns, however, do not have the capacity of names and nicknames to tell stories, but what pronouns can and cannot do has been of concern to Vizenor generally and in his autobiographies most particularly, where he has for long wrestled with the issue of pronominal self-reference.

In 1976, in his first autobiography, "I Know What You Mean, Erdupps MacChurbbs: Autobiographical Myths and Metaphors," Vizenor rather unproblematically wrote of himself as "I," a practice he continued in the brief self-portrait "Gerald Vizenor" in 1980. By 1987, however, in "Crows Written on the Poplars: Autocritical Autobiographies," he quoted the 1976 text extensively but referred to himself in both the third and the first person, announcing, "The first and third person personas are me"(101). The reader is to place this enunciation in relation to a categorization of autobiographies as "wild pastimes over the pronouns" (101). It was in that same text that Vizenor—I believe for the first time (he has used the quotation on a number of other occasions)—quoted Georges Gusdorf's observation: "Through most of human history, the individual does not oppose himself to all others; he does not feel himself to exist outside of others and still less against others, but very much *with* others in an interdependent existence that asserts its rhythms everywhere" (107). *Interior Landscapes*, Vizenor's book-length autobiography of 1990, repeats the subtitle of the 1976 piece—*Autobiographical Myths and Metaphors*—and reassumes the

---

9. This is included in Vizenor's 1994 collection *Manifest Manners*, and it is a revised version—perhaps I should say a parallel or alternative version—of an essay called "The Ruins of Representation: Shadow Survivance and the Literature of Dominance." Vizenor was kind enough to send me a manuscript of this essay dated November 1992, about the time, I imagine, he would have been sending the "Shadow Survivance" text to his publisher. Substantively, the two versions are very similar—especially in their commentary on pronouns, the matter of particular concern to me here—although phrasing varies, sometimes in ways that seem to make a semantic difference. A good deal of Vizenor's work is variably reiterative—Vizenor repeating and revising Vizenor—and a study of this dimension of his work is needed.

relatively unproblematic use of the "I" as Vizenor revisits and also revises his life as previously published.

The recent essay "Shadow Survivance" contains Vizenor's fullest commentary on the subject of pronouns. Vizenor offers a virtual windstorm of quotations—from Francis Jacques, Anthony Kenny, Harold Noonan, and Mikhail Bakhtin—relating to pronoun usage. All of these are presented largely without comment, or they are glossed by sentences that intentionally and, often, all-too-successfully resist secure comprehension. In any case, although it is not clear what Vizenor might actually *mean*, what he forcefully *signifies* is his sense that pronoun usage, in particular the use of the first-person singular, is a very risky business.

In "Shadow Survivance," Vizenor quotes Gusdorf again (95), asserts that "first person pronouns have no referents" (20), and one time speaks of himself in the third person ("Gerald Vizenor edited *Narrative Chance*") (15). He quotes Bakhtin's notebook observation: "The *I* hides in the other and in others . . . to cast from itself the burden of being the only *I* (I-for-myself) in the world" (103).[10] And he also quotes Kenny's question "Shall we say that 'I' is a demonstrative?"[11] But whatever "I" is, Vizenor is wary of it:

> The first person pronoun has never been the original absence of the heard, not even as the absence or transvaluation in the silence of a reader. . . . The personal, possessive, demonstrative, relative and interrogative pronouns are translations and transvaluations, the absence of names, presence, and consciousness heard in tribal stories.
>
> The pronoun endures as twice the absence of the heard, and more than the mere surrogate signifier or simulation in tribal stories. (*Manifest* 97)

Denying to first-person pronouns the status of "original absence of the heard," Vizenor reserves that status for the noun in writing. In *Dead Voices,*

---

10. In "The Ruins of Representation," Vizenor footnotes this quotation, giving the reference and offering some further quotation from Bakhtin. ("Shadow Survivance" has no notes, nor do any of the other essays in *Manifest Manners*, which, unlike most of Vizenor's other collections of essays, does have an index.) On the page before the remarks cited by Vizenor, Bakhtin wrote: "The history of autobiography (Misch). The heterogeneous composition of my image. *A person at the mirror. Not-I* in me; something larger than me in me" (146, first emphasis mine). These words seem available for contextualizing Bagese and the bear-in-the-mirror of *Dead Voices*, most particularly when reading *Dead Voices* in relation to autobiography.

11. I would answer that question with the observation that the "I" in any text is discursively engaged, like other demonstratives, in deixis. It is interesting to note that in Ducrot and Todorov's *Encyclopedic Dictionary*, the section on "demonstratives" immediately precedes that on "deictics."

he early on has Laundry note that Bagese tricks demons "with *dead* pronouns" (16, my emphasis), and in a text of the following year, a new
introduction to *Summer in the Spring: Anishinaabe Lyric Poems and Stories,* Vizenor speaks of "the ironic amusement of overstated personal pronouns" (10). And as he did in "Shadow Survivance" and "The Ruins of
Representation," he here, one time at least, evades the most "overstated"
pronoun of all, the "I," by writing of himself in the third person ("The
editor and interpreter of the dream songs and stories in this book has
heard songs and stories in anishinaabemowin [the Ojibwa language], but
he is not a primary speaker of a tribal language") (17–18).

The political dimension of Vizenor's hostility to the first-person singular becomes clear when we consider his remark, in *The People Named the
Chippewa,* directed against some members of the American Indian Movement: "The new radicals frown, even grimace at cameras, and *claim the
atrocities endured by all tribal cultures in first person pronouns*" (130, my
emphasis). How, then, is one to speak against "the atrocities endured by
all tribal cultures" in a tribal or communal fashion? For Vizenor, the answer will come in *Dead Voices,* with the decision to adopt the first-person
plural. But that decision requires first that he commit himself to fighting
for the survivance of tribal people with the pen rather than—as the "new
radicals" do—the sword or gun. Vizenor identifies himself as one whose
weapon of choice is the "wordarrow."

It is in *Interior Landscapes,* in a chapter called, "Avengers at Wounded
Knee," that Vizenor explicitly discovers and announces a turn away from
the gun. The chapter describes Vizenor's attendance at a "historic meeting" (235) at Calico Hall on the Pine Ridge Reservation, in February 1973
during the AIM occupation, and his intense reaction to the presence in a
small cabin of "more than a hundred tribal people from several tribes, from
cities and reservations" (235). "I was obsessed," Vizenor wrote, "with a
sense of spiritual warmth, and moved by the communal anticipation of the
tribal people there" (235). He noted his deep response to "the sound of
the drums, the drums, the drums"; then he went outside.

> I was liberated on the air, in the night sky, and said my name out loud,
> once, twice. . . . I had been close to my own truth, the absolute truth
> of spiritual conversion that night; a few more minutes, hours, and my
> name might have been lost to the tribe behind a bunker at Wounded
> Knee. I might have raised my rifle to that airplane over the village in
> the morning; instead, my pen was raised to terminal creeds. (235)

Preserving his "name," Vizenor also preserves pronominal self-reference in the first-person singular. As I have tried to show, however, his dissatisfaction with an "I" that arrogates to itself qualities of autonomy, individuality, and uniqueness—the qualities, of course, of the romantic and postromantic ego in the West—continues to grow.[12]

Inasmuch as names and nicknames, by means of the stories they tell, identify and link individuals to their communities, they have, for Vizenor, a force and efficacy that pronouns cannot and do not have. Pronouns "endure," as we have noted, as "twice the absence of the heard"; in writing, as we have noted, they are marked by secondariness, and Vizenor's loyalties are to speech as primary and to nouns. This romantic position stands in rather uneasy tension with Vizenor's admiration, here and elsewhere, of a certain Derridaean poststructuralism or Lyotardian postmodernism[13] for which writing is privileged over speech and for which names, inasmuch as they pretend to "natural" affinities with what they name, are acutely symptomatic of logocentric nostalgia.

This tension has a long and poignant history in Vizenor's work. For Vizenor is deeply attracted to an orality traditionally associated with collective or "tribal" identities and ancestral homelands. But he is also absolutely and unsentimentally clear about the present necessity of writing the oral tradition in the diasporic solitude of the cities. As Elaine Jahner perceptively noted in 1985, "at the beginning of his career, Vizenor saw all writing as an act that destroys the life of the oral exchange," claiming as late as 1984

---

12. Sympathetic as I am to Vizenor's critique of the Western, bourgeois, individualistic, often aggressive, and self-aggrandizing (male) ego and to his call for further exploration of the possibilities of plural self-reference, I would nonetheless call attention to an alternative line of thought about the "I" even in the West. Mieke Bal's essay "First Person, Second Person, Same Person: Narrative as Epistemology" raises many of the relevant issues; she urges that we distinguish "autonomy from individualism" (301), noting the complementarity between first- and second-person pronouns (307) and, consistent with the remarks I cited above from Ducrot and Todorov, the "dependency on others" (301) of first-person usage. Lejeune too points to the fact that " 'Identity' is a *constant relationship* between the one and the many" ("Autobiography in the Third Person" 34), citing Paul Valéry's observation that "the individual is a dialogue." There is also the formula of Rimbaud, "Je est un autre" ("I is another"), which connects to the later Bakhtin, cited by Vizenor and cited above, who wonders, "To what degree is it possible to combine *I* and *other* in one neutral image of person?" (Bakhtin, 146–47).

13. In an essay called " 'The Last of the Oral Tradition in Electronic Word Processing': Traditional Material and Postmodern Form in Gerald Vizenor's *Bearheart*," Wolfgang Hochbruck offers some insights into the split that I have called romantic and postmodern, Hochbruck's term "traditional" parallels my use of "romantic." Hochbruck also—although only briefly—distinguishes between "Lyotard's harmless language games" and Vizenor's " 'word wars' between different cultures" (89). As I have argued in chapter 3, Vizenor's postmodern stance can be misleading; his postmodernism, to recall Appiah, may be an antagonist as much as an ally of Western postmodernism.

that printed stories alter tribal experience (in Blaeser in press). Nonetheless, Jahner continued, "over time he has come to a more accepting view of what writing is and can be" (in Blaeser in press)—provided, of course, that the writing be of the type that, in a phrase of Julia Kristeva's, "breaks out of the rules of a language censored by grammar and semantics" (in Hochbruck 98). Thus Vizenor's attempt to write the oral tradition, as Wolfgang Hochbruck shrewdly notes, "does not replace the monological form of colonial discourse with an equally monological romantic myth about what is or what is not Indian."[14] For him, the oral tradition "has for the most part become one of many bits and pieces in a postmodern language game" (Hochbruck 93).

But this is not "only" a game; rather, like the wanaki game of *Dead Voices*, it is a chance at peace. As we have noted in *The Heirs of Columbus*, Vizenor wants—traditionally, romantically, or even in Sartrean left-modernist fashion—his postmodernist, fragmented oral writing to serve the unifying, communal-cohesive, and "healing" functions he associates with traditional orality. Just as Vizenor insists, in Robert Silverman's words, "that the trickster [can] be defined as compassionate rather than amoral and asocial, as Paul Radin described him," a "kind of necessary fiction" (15), so too must he insist that trickster discourse can be consistent functionally with an oral tradition that, both in the present and in the past, is marked by a certain groundedness (e.g., expectations are fulfilled rather than subverted, and ironies are of the satiric sort, focused and limited). This insistence, it seems to me, is also a necessary fiction.[15] For all

---

14. In a fine discussion of Vizenor's "Postindian Warriors" (in *Manifest Manners*), Michael Elliott shows that the repeated refrain "This portrait is not an Indian" allows for the presumption that other portraits might actually *be* an Indian, something Vizenor has sought to disallow. See Elliott, "The Next-to-Last-Lecture."

15. To call it a fiction is not to call it false or devoid of usefulness. This is Andrew Wiget's error in a harsh but importantly corrective review of Vizenor's edited volume *Narrative Chance*. Wiget points to the fundamental unsuitability of postmodern discourse and deconstruction "for elucidating *oral* literatures" ("Review" 477). I believe Wiget is correct: but Vizenor's own use of the oral tradition is very much, in Hochbruck's phrase, "the adoption"— or, as I should say, the *invention*, in the sense of Eric Hobsbawm and Terence Ranger—"of a cultural image rather than an experienced life-form" ("Last of the Oral Tradition," 91). It is (Hochbruck once more) "fabricated orality" (90), a paradoxical or catachrestical conjunction of the romantic and the postmodern. Wiget's critique of Vizenor's trickster is also technically correct, as when he writes that historically, "Native Americans have pointed to the trickster to explain certain aspects of perceived reality or to justify a proposed course of action" ("Review," 478), a function that an "absence" (as Vizenor refers to the trickster in *Narrative Chance*) or a sign that engages in the "perpetual deferral of signification" (478) could never perform. But Vizenor's trickster is also an invention, a "necessary fiction," in

the wild and wonderful ironies and language games, *Dead Voices*, similar to *The Heirs of Columbus*, returns in the end to the old and moving values of communal cohesion and survivance.[16] *Dead Voices*, like *The Heirs*, employs an apparently postmodernist manner in the interest of left-modernist or (neo-)humanist interests.

Indeed, *Dead Voices* concludes with the strongest defense Vizenor has yet provided of the necessity of writing the oral tradition in the urban post-Indian era in the interest of healing and survivance. In the remainder of this essay, I will try to show how he moves to this defense of written storytelling (a quite personal statement, it seems to me) with reference to the matters we have taken up thus far—names, nicknames, pronouns, pens, and guns—and, also, squirrels.

Having three times tired "I," and once "I" and "he" in his autobiographical writing, Vizenor, in *Dead Voices*, has Laundry provisionally settle on "we," a move from metonymic to synecdochic self-reference. As I have shown elsewhere, this is a move quite typical of Native American writers of autobiography.[17] My claim is that the shift from "I" to "we" in *Dead Voices* bears as much on Gerald Vizenor's sense of identity as it does on that of a fictional character nicknamed Laundry.

The final words of *Dead Voices*, as I have said, are "We must go on." Spoken by Laundry, these words are a quotation from Bagese, who has several times said "We must go on" (62, 135, 139ff) with reference to the

---

Silverman's phrase from Wallace Stevens. It will not—Wiget's point, with which I agree—aid us in understanding the tricksters of the oral tradition. But it may very well be valuable as a *metaphor* in those texts that give us "the oral tradition in electronic word processing" (Hochbruck, "Last of the Oral Tradition"). This possibility Wiget, at least in the review I have cited, does not seem to appreciate. Louis Owens, in *Other Destinies*, as noted in the last chapter, has thoughtfully wrestled with these issues.

16. Cf. Hochbruck on *Bearheart*: "In the end, only the speakers of a tribal language in a positive oral tradition survive" ("Last of the Oral Tradition," 97); "among the survivors are not only four people but also a swarm of seven shaman crows and one dog" (98); and "Vizenor's postmodern novel suddenly exposes an open flank to a possible romantic reading of the whole story as an escape and (re-)creation myth" (99). It is in the recent *Manifest Manners* that Vizenor's instantiation of the term *survivance* as a challenge to the colonial discourse of dominance has its most powerful effect. Here it becomes apparent that survivance is not a term set in opposition to dominance (*subordination* or *subservience* would be the antithetical terms) in a manner that would seek to reverse the outcome of history while leaving the terms of historical contest (as, of course, established by the victors) in place. Rather, the substitution of *survivance* for *dominance* seeks to alter the terms of Euramerican–Native American relations—and, of course, to animate alternative outcomes, in much the same way that Silko does in her *Almanac of the Dead* (see above).

17. See Krupat, "Native American Autobiography and the Synecdochic Self."

importance of stories to the survivance of tribal people. But these words
also refer to Samuel Beckett, whose conclusion to his novel *The Unnam-
able* serves as the first of three epigraphs to *Dead Voices*. And it is not
Bagese or Laundry but Gerald Vizenor who has seen to it that Beckett's
words—"I can't go on, I'll go on"—echo in the novel, and it is Vizenor
who has caused them to echo with a difference.[18] For Bagese's "We must
go on" transforms Beckett's first-person singular to the plural, as it also
changes his auxiliary verb "will"—in contraction (in translation)—an enunciation of purpose or intention, to "must," an enunciation of necessity.

So we might say that *Dead Voices*, a story about stories, tells a tale
of the hunt for pronouns, for some provisionally acceptable, pronominal
"shadow writing" of the tribally *spoken* name or nickname. To speak of
the hunt for pronouns in *Dead Voices* is once more to foreground the issue
of Vizenor's commitment to word hunting rather than man or, as I want to
show now, animal hunting. This commitment has been abundantly documented in Vizenor's autobiographical texts, in particular "Crows Written
on the Poplars," in which Vizenor writes of himself in the third person,
noting he "has pretended to be a hunter in his stories, . . . but he has
never had to track an animal to the end, as he would to the last pronoun
in his stories, to feed his families and friends" (105). Vizenor is commenting here on an incident that occurred in 1956 (or 1957); described in his
first autobiography, "I Know What You Mean, Erdupps MacChurbbs," it
is repeated in three of his four autobiographical texts. (It is omitted only
from the brief 1980 account, "Gerald Vizenor.")

In "1956: In a Low Voice without Words," the penultimate section of
"I Know What You Mean, Erdupps MacChurbbs," Vizenor tells of hunting a large red squirrel in the woods of Minnesota. His first shot shattered
the squirrel's shoulder bone; a second shot "tore the flesh and fur away
from the top of his skull"; a third "tore his lower jaw away"; and a fourth
and final shot "shattered his forehead" (107). As this animal, "who wanted
to live more than anything" Vizenor had ever known (107), finally died,
Vizenor asked his forgiveness, wept, and sang "a slow death song in a low
voice without words until it was dark" (108).

This moving story is central to "Crows Written on the Poplars," which
is, at the outset, announced as "a mixedblood autobiographical causerie
and a narrative on the slow death of a common red squirrel" (101). Vizenor

---

18. In the preceding chapter, we noted as well Vizenor's responsibility for the lengthy
quotation from Sartre. It will have escaped no one that for all their differences, Beckett and
Sartre share a certain generational and intellectual formation.

quotes selected passages from the account of the killing of the squirrel in "Erdupps MacChurbbs" and comments on them, speaking of himself in the third person. Thus, for example, he wrote: "The slow death of the squirrel burned in his memories; he sold his rifles and never hunted animals. Instead he told stories about squirrels" (105–6). Refusing "to accept the world as a hunter" (106), Vizenor says that he became, instead, a "word hunter" (106).

He returns to the story of the squirrel in *Interior Landscapes* in the brief chapter called "October 1957: Death Song to a Red Rodent." Here he does not quote but slightly revises his earlier account, now suggesting that the "red squirrel *dared* Vizenor to hunt him" (168, my emphasis) and characterizing himself as an *urban* hunter (167–68). In some regards distancing himself from the squirrel—by referring to the animal as a "rodent," by writing short, terse sentences, by interrupting the narrative with quotations, and by suggesting that the squirrel "dared" the hunter—Vizenor here also brings himself closer to the squirrel—by remarking, after the first shot, "I understood his instinct to escape; in a dream *we* reached up with *our* right paw" (168, my emphasis), and by stating, "I owe so much to that red squirrel who dared me to hunt him in the oaks, *who died in me*" (170, my emphasis). The chapter concludes: "I sold my rifle and never hunted to kill animals or birds again. The violent death of a wild animal caused by my weapon was a separation from the natural world, not a reunion. I would defend squirrels and comfort them in death; that would be the natural human response. I would not shoot an animal again unless my life depended on the hunt" (170).

The story of the hunting of the red squirrel reappears in *Dead Voices*. In the chapter dated June 1979, Bagese turns the third of the wanaki cards and says, "We are squirrels" (60). She then tells a story about a tribal hunter who "raised his small calibre rifle, took aim, and fired at a stout red squirrel" (64). And, in slow and detailed fashion, the story, as the reader has come to know it from Gerald Vizenor's autobiographies, unfolds again; only this time, the story is told from the point of view of the squirrel. Vizenor here imagines a literal conjunction, not a separation of the human and animal, but this union is possible only for Bagese, not for Laundry.

In 1976 Vizenor, noting the "squirrels . . . eating without fear and jumping from tree to tree" ("I Know" 107), had written the sentence, "I was jumping with them but against them as the hunter" ("I Know" 107). He comments on this passage in 1987: "Here, in the last sentence, he pretends to be an arboreal animal, a romantic weakness; he was neither a hunter nor a tribal witness to the hunt. He was there as a mixedblood writer, in a

transitive confessional, then and now, in his imaginative autobiographies"
("Crows" 105). Vizenor will no longer allow this sort of "natural" or
"romantic" union with animals to himself or to Laundry—although, as
I have said, he does permit it to Bagese, very much a "tribal witness" (e.g.,
Bagese says, "We are squirrels out on a thin branch, and we run at dawn
with the leaves" [*Dead Voices* 59]). Laundry's connection to animals, his
"reunion" with rather than "separation from the natural world" (*Dead
Voices* 170), perhaps like Vizenor's own, must finally come through the
adoption of Bagese's plural first-person pronoun in writing. (As when, for
example, Bagese notes, "The plural pronoun *we* is used to be sure nature
is not separated from humans" [*Dead Voices* 28]).

The "same" red squirrel, then, appears in the "same" story in *Dead
Voices*, but with a difference, one that involves a name and a pronoun. For
the red squirrel of *Dead Voices* is named (nicknamed?) Ducks, and Ducks
is not male and pronominally referred to as "he" (as was the case in the
earlier accounts) but is female and so is pronominally referred to as "she."
(E.g., the first bullet "shattered the bone in her shoulder" [65].) Just as
Gerald Vizenor, the young hunter, had done in his autobiographical accounts, so the hunter in *Dead Voices* "cried, and . . . sang a slow death song
without words until it was dark" (67). But here Vizenor the word-hunter
once again turns "autocritical," perhaps even indicating a dissatisfaction
with or an incompleteness to his treatment of this part of his life in his
earlier autobiographical writing. For Bagese (who, recall, is one with the
squirrels) says, "The hunter wanted to believe that he was forgiven, but
his stories were dead voices" (67).

In time, however, the hunter *is* forgiven after he tries to save a red squirrel hit by a car in the city. Such an event was, indeed, briefly mentioned in
"Crows Written on the Poplars" (cf. 106), but it is expanded and given a
very particular emphasis in *Dead Voices* as the hunter repeats, in the city,
the actions he had once performed in the woods: "He stretched out beside the squirrel, touched his head and paws, and sang a death song" (68).
"The hunter was forgiven at last in the city" (68).

Bagese shares Vizenor's view that the cities must become the sanctuar-
ies for many tribal people because, as she says, "the tribes are dead" (134),
having become "dead voices" (136). But she presents the case in her final
monologue, dated January 1980: "There is nothing more to be done with
our voices in the cities" (134). With a poignant, elegiac lyricism reminiscent
perhaps of Beckett, she repeats the phrase "We must go on," although for
her, the animals are now "in the eye and our voices are dead" (136), "our
stories . . . removed with the animals" (137). If the only way the tribal voice

can be heard in the city is textually (e.g., it can only be *seen*, not heard) and if stories in print are only dead voices, then we are at a tragic impasse. Twice more Bagese affirms, "We must go on" (139, 140). But she herself does not go on—rather, as we have noted, she becomes a bear, *makwa*, the most powerful of animals to the Anishinaabe. But she cannot solve the problem of how to produce a living, healing voice in the interest of tribal survivance in the cities.

It remains for Laundry to respond to Bagese, and his response, the replacement of Bagese's tragic story with a comic narrative of Native American survivance, is entirely consistent with Vizenor's regularly repeated sense of the function of the Native American writer today. Laundry "waited a few more years and then decided that the stories [Bagese had] told [him] must be published" (143). Although he had initially agreed to refrain from publishing Bagese's stories, he changed his mind in a manner that parallels Vizenor's own thinking. With *Dead Voices*, Vizenor seems to have moved not merely to an acceptance of writing but to a firm defense of it. He has Laundry conclude the novel with an address to Bagese: "Bagese, these published stories are the same as the wanaki pictures and stones that you place in your apartment to remember the earth, the traces of birds and animals near the lake. I am with you in the mirror, and hold a stone in my pocket, the stone you left for me on the table, to remember your stories. We must go on" (144).

Referring to himself plurally, synecdochically, communally, and tribally, Laundry accepts Bagese's stories about animals as his own and takes responsibility for publishing them in the interest of the people's survivance. We must go on, he says, echoing Bagese and altering Beckett to settle on the pronoun that Gerald Vizenor himself might choose; if not so good as a name or a nickname, the pronoun is at least the best choice available to a writer of stories in the oral tradition. *Dead Voices*, a novel and readable as "fiction" from a Euramerican perspective, may well, from a Native American perspective, also be read as autobiography, as a "true" account of Gerald Vizenor's experience as a mixed-blood writer, an account that documents an engagement and a trajectory that are not for him alone.

5

A Nice Jewish Boy among the Indians

WHO ARE YOU, WHO ARE YOU? IDENTITY QUESTIONS ARE EVERYWHERE today, and the answers, out in the world, can have very extreme consequences: Tutsi or Hutu, Shiite or Sunni, Catholic or Protestant. My undergraduate student Dalila Suhonjic recently wrote, "I am a Bosnian Muslim, but prefer to simply be called a Bosnian because that is my identity." Her preference was not, however, permitted. Because others preferred to identify her as a Bosnian Muslim, she had been forced to leave the University of Zagreb in Croatia and then her home in Gradiska, Bosnia. Her parents' house was shelled twice and then taken over by their neighbors. The family was given twenty-four hours to leave the country. Dalila believes that eleven of her high school classmates are dead; others are safe in one part of the world or another; the fate of many is not clear. Dalila continued: "There are many Bosnian Croats and Bosnian Serbs who also prefer to simply be called Bosnians. They believe in multicultural Bosnia as do I. This is our shared identity, and what makes us different from other former Yugoslavians. But we are not allowed to believe in this." Our shared identity—that which makes us different . . .

We are most certainly allowed to believe in multiculturalism in the academy; I am on record as being "for" it in the interest of an imagined global community, even though I now understand how multiculturalism may simply be the cultural logic of transnational capitalism, more adept than an older Eurocentrism at producing not the universal man of humanism but the universal consumer.

In the First World academy, as Arif Dirlik wrote, "fragmentation of earlier metanarratives appears benign . . . for its promise of more democratic, multicultural, and cosmopolitan epistemologies. In the world outside the academy, however, it shows in murderous ethnic conflict." But that doesn't necessarily mean that Dalila and I must give up all hope that the "benign" multiculturalism and cosmopolitanism of academics might still have some "real" effect in the world outside the academy.

Who am I? I know who I'm *not*: I'm not—although the Lakota filmmaker, Harriet Skye, at dinner one evening thought I might be—a Navajo. Nor am I a Lakota, Seneca, Cheyenne, or Paiute; I'm not a Native American, not an Indian. Doing what I do, however, prompts questions about my "tribe" or "nation" more frequently these days than in the late 1970s, when I first began to publish on Native American literature. Now, as Linda Alcoff notes of one Canadian case, "white" critics are being asked by some Native people to "move over," to leave the field to those who *are* what they write about. I've already argued that, from an ethical and an epistemological point of view, it makes no sense to exclude any would-be participant from the critical conversations that make up the contemporary interpretation of Native American literatures. Nor does it make sense politically to reject the aid of allies just because they are not "us."

No, I'm not an Indian. I'm a Jew, the son of working-class Jewish immigrants. But I "do" Native American literature. In this chapter I want to explore the relationship between identity and vocation, the ways in which "Who I am" is related to "What I do." "In my beginning is my end," T. S. Eliot wrote at the beginning of "East Coker," second of the *Four Quartets*; he concluded, "In my end is my beginning." Eliot speaks religiously, in terms of syntheses and samenesses; I work in a secular manner, in terms of analyses and differences. But there is something to what Eliot wrote, and I'll try to say some things about my beginnings and my—at least my vocational—ends.

Until I was almost five years old, my family lived with my grandmother, my mother's mother. My grandmother could not read or write any language—not Yiddish, her first and best language, not Russian, her second language, and not English, her awkward third language. We would all gather around the kitchen table every payday to help my grandmother sign her name to the salary check she received for her work in a New York sweatshop sewing silk linings into fur coats. I remember marveling at how long this took and

how difficult it seemed to be for her to form the letters that would identify her to the bank. Before I was five, I could write my name—print it,
anyway—almost as well as she could write hers, or so I thought. And I had
many times been told that once I went to school, I would quickly learn to
manage my letters more and more skillfully. Yet my grandmother seemed
to make no progress; each time she took the pen to her paycheck, she
proceeded just as slowly, just as laboriously, as the time before. My grandmother was one of the first people I knew in the world, and she was a
person from an oral culture. But I didn't learn the richness of orality from
my grandmother; instead, I learned only the pain of illiteracy, how it could
hurt to be without writing.

The Acoma poet Simon Ortiz notes that the "oral tradition evokes and
expresses a belief system, and it is specific activity"—such things, for example, as "the interaction of the grandfather with his grandson"—"that
confirms and conveys that belief." Simon and I were born in the same year,
1941, and Simon's work has been important to me, but our relations to
our grandparents were very different.

My grandmother, as I have said, most certainly came from an oral culture, but I don't know what her "belief system" actually was. She lit candles
for the Shabbat every Friday night and then went in to her room, where
she would look at a photo of her deceased husband, my grandfather, and
cry quietly. My grandmother was not a storyteller; the kind of grandparent-
grandchild "interaction" that Simon Ortiz refers to didn't exist between
us. I never heard a traditional Yiddish tale of dybbuks and inspired rebbes
from my grandmother's mouth; I never knew there were such tales until I
read them in books.

> *"But maybe she told those stories in the old country. Maybe it was
> displacement that silenced her here."*

Simon wrote that the language he heard "from birth to six years of age
in the Acoma family and community was the basis and source of all [he]
would do later." But Yiddish does not play the role for me that Aacqumeh
did for Simon. If there was anything left of an earlier and quite rich Yiddish cultural life on the Lower East Side, I was entirely unaware of it,
growing up in the 1940s and 1950s. I think it was sometime in the mid-
1980s that Abe Lebewohl, a concentration camp survivor and the owner
of the Second Avenue Deli, set into the concrete sidewalk in front of his
establishment a series of stars and the names of the great performers of the
Second Avenue Yiddish theater. But as a boy, I knew virtually nothing of
this. I fled Yiddish for English as rapidly as I could, and in the family circle,

as far back as I can remember, when spoken to in Yiddish I would answer only in English. Later, I would aspire to French, and once in Paris, in the rue des Rosiers, in the Jewish quarter, I would admit, in French, to an old man who spoke to me in Yiddish that, yes, it was true, I was an American Jew whose French was far better than my Yiddish.

> *"But lots of French Jews also refused to have anything to do with Yiddish. And an older generation of Indians certainly were antiblanket and wouldn't talk Indian."*

> *"Just think of the autobiography of Emmy Valandry, that I told you about. She had a Lakota mother and a white soldier father. She turned into someone in violent rebellion against her ethnic background."*

My grandmother not only did not tell folk stories but also did not tell of her personal, historical experience. Perhaps that would have been too painful, for some small part of her experience—the experience of violence and oppression, which I learned about late and sketchily from my mother—roughly parallels the historical experience of some Native Americans. My grandmother fled Russia immediately after her husband, not yet thirty years old, had died of typhus, a disease he had contracted while fleeing a pogrom. The mounted cossacks who hunted and tormented him, the drunken civilians who beat him and left him for dead, did so, for the most part, simply because he was a Jew. Although the comparison isn't quite exact, still I imagine those cossacks and drunken Russian citizens as not so very different from Col. John Chivington and his men at Sand Creek, from the cavalry at the Washita River, and too many other places even to mention, from those who killed Indians, for the most part, simply because they were Indians. Pogroms occurred in the Ukraine, my grandmother's region, as elsewhere in greater Russia, with a certain irregular regularity. On this particular occasion, the one that would lead to my grandfather's death, my grandmother grabbed up her two very young daughters, my mother and her younger sister, my aunt, and hid under the hay in a neighbor's barn until the marauders left. Wouldn't she have felt the same fear that Cheyenne and Lakota women had felt hiding with their children from raiding soldiers?

> *"After the 22d of June 1941 when the war in the Soviet Union began, the Jews in Latvia were slaughtered by the Nazis. There were Jewish ghettos in Riga and Daugarpils where my parents lived. The Jews were transported to the suburbs of the city and slaughtered. . . . On July 8, 1941, Jews came to a synagogue to pray. The Nazis burnt the synagogue and all the people inside died. There were many Latvians who helped the Nazis slaughter the Jews.*

*I was then in Riga studying and it was impossible to return home. I
went on foot toward Russia, and reached the town of Pskov. I worked
building tanks until I was fired when it was learned that I had relatives in the U.S. It was only at the end of 1945 that I could get back
home. I found that all my family had been slaughtered in the ghetto.
My younger brother Faivesh—he was eight—had left the ghetto with
his friends to try to find food. A guard caught him and shot him. My
sister was a beautiful woman, she even won a title, Miss Daugarpils, at
the local beauty contest. She, too, they all were killed."*

Just as Native women did, my grandmother also kept her little girls quiet,
and they were not discovered. But when she learned of her husband's
death, she did not, as the books tell me the Native women did, seek out
her relatives; instead, she gathered what she could, took her two girls,
and set out overland from Skverer, the ghetto town outside of Kiev in the
Ukraine where she had been born, across Russia, coming eventually to the
Netherlands.

There she met a man from a town near her own. He had in his possession whatever papers were required to come to America. The papers he
had were for himself, his wife, and his two daughters. But the wife and the
two daughters had died on the journey. My grandmother had no papers,
and it seems she made an arrangement with this man: they would marry
and pretend her children were his daughters, the daughters named on his
papers. That way, she could settle in America. In return, she would pay
him a certain amount of money for a certain number of years. Apparently
they never lived together as husband and wife—

*"Maybe he was a rapist, maybe he was a monster. Did you ask? Did you
really try to find out? Sounds like the poor woman was traumatized!"*

—and apparently she paid off her debt by sweatshop work over many long
years. My mother says he was not a good man. That is all I know.

My grandmother never told of these things any more than she told
traditional Yiddish stories. The admonition of the Holocaust survivors to
bear witness and speak so that the world would never forget did not make
its way to our house. My grandmother, who prayed and cried to her husband's photograph every Friday night, was ashamed that she had married
another man, no matter that her action had saved her life and the lives of
her children.

I learned the little that I know only when I was in college, when, vaguely
aware of something coming to be called "oral history" and with a new interest in documenting family and local traditions, I pressed my mother for
information. What, exactly, were these papers? How much did my grand-

mother pay, and how long did she pay it? Whatever became of this man? How long did it take to get from the Ukraine to the Netherlands? How long were they there? What did they eat? Where did they stay? How did they communicate with the Dutch? My mother didn't know, and as I have said, my grandmother never spoke of these things to me. I never questioned her directly; the few times I tiptoed toward these matters, she scared me off—or I got scared and didn't press the issue. No, I suppose I didn't ask, at least not persistently enough. My grandmother could not read or write; for the most part she spoke a language other than English; she had suffered great oppression. Yet she did not play the role for me that Simon Ortiz's grandfather did for him. Simon always knew that he was Aacqumeh; his dilemma was how best to continue to be Aacqumeh in a world of powerful Mericanos. What it meant to be Aacqumeh, as I understand Simon Ortiz, was not seriously in question.

> "O.K., Simon has made his peace with all this, but there are dozens of Acomas who—maybe like you?—have not."

> "But what about the many Rockies, i.e., in Silko's Ceremony, working, say, for the BIA? Or the Ben Nighthorse Campbells, or the myriad other Native Americans who saw America as offering the same opportunities—including escape from tradition—that you have described for non-natives. And the unenrolled, the happily detribalized, the willingly assimilated and American Indians? Don't forget about them."

I knew that I was Jewish, but I didn't know what that might mean, especially as I increasingly came to feel myself to be "American." In this regard, my own situation, if I seek to compare it with that of Native Americans, more nearly recalls that of an earlier generation; it resembles the situation of people, say, like Charles Alexander Eastman (Ohiyesa) or Gertrude Bonnin (Zitkala-Ša), people trying to be both "Indian" and "American," than it does that of people like Simon Ortiz.

But my situation is different from theirs too, and this is for historical as well as cultural reasons. No one today has explored these issues more acutely than Gerald Vizenor, and despite the great differences in our formations and temperaments, I find his meditations on "post-" identities extremely interesting. How is any one of us to acknowledge the many things that are just "given"—what Werner Sollors refers to as matters of "descent" rather than "consent"—and still allow room for the construction of consensual, even invented identities? As it happens, Vizenor and I, though not born in the same year, were born on the same day in October.

My father said very little; his father was silenced, murdered before Gerald was two. Vizenor and I both grew up in cities, where the past is hard to find.

Identity, of course, is a matter not only of reclaiming the past but also of responding to the present, to the social, historical, and political forces that construct the "Indian" or the "Jew" or, indeed, the "Aacqumeh" person in a variety of ways. Vizenor's postindian, he insists, is "postmodern," which for him seems to have something to do with the priority of imagination, of tribal and local stories rather than master narratives, and of what he calls survivance as a value set against the commitment to dominance of the West. Is Vizenor a postindian Indian? Am I a post-Jewish Jew? What would the "post" mean here?

So far as I can tell, my intellectual identity is more nearly a modern than a postmodern identity, to the extent, that is, that I want—anachronistically, as I have acknowledged—to make sense of things: books, the world, things like that. Some version of this "making sense" is, for me, the function of criticism, what I try to do. It's how I am and, thus, in good measure, who I am.

Simon speaks of the way in which colonized people come if not to despise, at least to look down on their own cultural achievements or values. His Aacqumeh Hano, Acoma people, as he has written, seemed very poor and very powerless in comparison with the Mericanos, the numerous and "rich" Americans. Linda Hogan has said similar things. She wrote: "I come from people who have not had privilege. This is because of our histories. Those who are privileged would like for us to believe that we are in some way defective, that we are not smart enough, not good enough." Smartness aside—I was a firstborn Jewish son and so automatically a *chuchem* (the *ch*'s are gutturals), a smart one—I felt the same sorts of things about the Jewish people around me, family and family friends. This, I now know, is a matter of class, and class, in these regards, cuts across (it does not transcend) race and culture and even, to some extent, gender. My family and their friends were all immigrants or the children of immigrants, people far removed from the Rothschilds or Lehmans, the Bergdorfs, Goodmans, or Bloomingdales, the Warner Brothers, or Foxes. They all were—to cite the title of Mike Gold's fictionalized autobiography, a book I did not know until long after I had graduated from college—"Jews without money."

They were also Jews without much formal schooling; my people did not go to City College in its glory days with Irving Howe and Sidney Hook. The passionate discussions among socialists and Zionists, Trotskyites and anarchists—discussions that Grace Paley, Sol Yurick, Ed Doctorow, Tillie

Olsen, and many other American Jewish writers have remembered from their childhoods—did not occur at our house. In comparison with the Americans, my people seemed to me deficient—decent, hardworking, and worthy of respect, to be sure, but not very interesting. The harsh and admittedly arrogant judgment of my adolescent self was that mine were a people not only without privilege, not only without money or education, but also virtually without culture.

> *"This hardly sounds like you're such a nice Jewish boy. This and some of what you say later sounds like you're writing out of a lot of unresolved resentment."*

There is no people without culture, of course, any more than there is a people without history. But as a child and young man, I did not have the anthropological conception of culture. Rather, in the absence of any positive sense of Jewish culture—no stories, no personal histories, no animated life of the cafes and restaurants described by Emma Goldman, Mike Gold, and Abraham Cahan—and with a religious schooling that, as I shall describe it below, seemed to me repulsive, "culture," for me, came to mean High Culture: classical music, paintings in museums, "difficult" poetry, cloth napkins, and more than one fork beside one's plate. For those like myself who were not born into it, High Culture could be obtained—this was the great promise of America, after all—first by diligent study, by *reading*, and then by attendance at an institution of higher learning. This meant that, unlike my relatives and their friends, I would have to go to college.

That a firstborn son of working-class Jewish immigrants should go to college seemed altogether unproblematic when I was growing up in the 1940s and 1950s.

> *"Well, isn't that a clear effect of culture? If you understood that going to college was what a nice Jewish boy should do, then you internalized a cultural expectation, no?"*

If you were smart—and just find me an American Jewish boy whose parents and grandparents don't think he's smart!—you would get through college. For a New York Jew there was, at worst, City College, which was free in those days and still very good, although in my family's understanding, anything free could only be worth its price. And there was, at best, even the Ivy League, for we did not know there were quotas for Jews, though we did know there were scholarships (*not* "financial aid") for the hardworking bright. So I went to school with good cheer, wishing not so much to turn myself into a goyish Mericano (house, car, money, table manners, and 2.3

children) as a—what?—a writer, I suppose. I shared that dream with Simon Ortiz and Gerald Vizenor, with Betty Louise Bell and Louis Owens, and with other Native Americans from a world in which writing seemed a way to participate in a bigger world. My precocious Francophilia led me to romanticize the status of expatriate writer; I most preferred Paris, of course, even though I increasingly came to feel that I would be an expatriate just about anywhere in America other than New York. But first I had to go to school.

For Native Americans, going to school was often a nightmarish experience. If Americans were really interested in "captivity narratives," as several Native people have remarked, then they should check out stories about the boarding schools; those stories would make the tales of Mary Rowlandson and Hannah Dustin literally pale. The Phoenix Indian School was not the only one to use a ball and chain, and the beatings and humiliations that Indian children endured or succumbed to (suicides were not infrequent) continued until very recently, until the seventies, the *nineteen*-seventies. (Just ask Mary Crow Dog or Anthony Apakark Thrasher, among others.) This is part of the Native American holocaust, and this holocaust too must be spoken and written, made known, so that the world can never forget.

For all of that (and it is much, and I will come back to it), some who went away to the schools—Jason Betzinez, who knew Geronimo, Zitkala-Ša (Gertrude Bonnin), Ohiyesa (Charles Alexander Eastman), Dr. Carlos Montezuma, and Helen Sekaquaptewa, among others—felt that they had learned things useful for themselves and for their people. Even though the reading and writing scenes that play so powerful a part in African American autobiography from at least Frederick Douglass to Malcolm X are absent from the texts of Native American writers and even though there is no "ascent to literacy" for a people committed to the ongoing vitality of an oral tradition, nonetheless, being able to read and to write (in English) was important to many Native intellectuals and artists. It was important to Simon Ortiz, for example. Luci Tapahonso, now trying to write in Navajo, first came to express herself poetically in English. This is true as well for Ofelia Zepeda, a Tohono O'odham linguist, for the Mesquakie poet Ray Young Bear, and, I imagine, even for Rex Lee Jim, whose Princeton education did not prevent him from writing poems in the Navajo language.

The mixed-blood Pomo writer and critic Greg Sarris (Sarris is also part Jewish) has recently reminded us of how *different* the Anglo school environment is from the home environment of many Native children and older students. For him, that difference is something to be minimized; his focus is on the traumatic effects of a movement from what is uniformly (and rather sentimentally) taken to be a homelife of warmth and nurturance to a coldly rationalized school-life—to, for example, physical placement by size or alphabetization, fixed mealtimes, formal requests to go to the toilet, and so on. His point is important, yet Sarris cannot or will not acknowledge the ways in which the rationalized classroom might be a relief to some young people, a welcome refuge from a kin-closeness that just might be experienced less positively—experienced, for example, as constraining, even very nearly suffocating. I am speaking of my own sense of these things, of course, but I don't think I'm entirely alone here. You don't have to be a Ricardo-turned-Richard Rodriguez (his reaction against his background seems to me the classic reaction of the colonized person) to feel exhilarated on discovering that it might actually be possible to *choose* one's identity, to construct or invent it—not evading but also not being limited by the givens of descent. I did not feel quite the revulsion against "tribalism" that the Tunisian Jew Albert Memmi did. Memmi wrote: "I discovered tribal life and learned to hate it. . . . This atmosphere of wrangling at home, the pettiness of our tribal community, its futile arguments and treacherous or even friendly gossip, . . . with everybody watched by everyone else, . . . all of it certainly contributed a lot to the feeling of being stifled that soon overcame me at home." But I felt something not very far from that.

> "Is it worth pointing out that 'gossip' is a key feature of much social control in the Pueblos? Along with witchcraft accusations, 'gossip' is a pervasive feature of intrafamilial discourse at Hopi and in many other Native societies (e.g., among the Navajo)."

It was only by leaving the "tribe," I came to believe, that I could ever be myself, whoever I might be.

> "Yet you don't feel this in any way inhibits the kind of criticism and analysis you do of Indian writing? It might be wise to address this issue more directly."

Kin and family for me were made up of the constant bickering of three women and the silence of one man. My mother, my aunt (my mother's younger sister), and my grandmother were constantly arguing with each other. Some of it may have been a way of expressing affection; perhaps in comparison with the coolness and constraint of the stereotypical WASP family, it might even have had a certain ethnic charm. But to my increasingly "American" set of values—which longed for at least the facade of politeness and civility, however frosty—the things my grandmother said to my mother and, in particular, to my aunt (who was hopelessly unworthy of any consideration whatever because she was not married) were frightening. And my father said hardly a word.

Yet my father was—how could it be otherwise?—very important to me. Of the four children in his family, he was the third born and the only boy. He was a good athlete, a strong swimmer. Working as a lifeguard at a borscht belt resort in the Jewish Catskills one summer, my father had saved a man and his son from drowning after their canoe had capsized on the local lake. He received a reward for that act: a check for five cents. He never cashed it. I keep it in my wallet. My father loved the water, but it terrified my inland mother and my grandmother. I never learned to swim.

At five feet eight inches tall, my father was a basketball star for Franklin K. Lane High School in Brooklyn, where he grew up. His modest dream was to be a gym teacher, and he enrolled, perhaps with some small aid from a basketball scholarship, at a college that specialized in producing "p.t."—physical training—instructors. Its curious name was Savage. Most of the stories I've heard from those days tell how Jewish parents scrimped and saved and suppressed the aspirations of the daughters so that the son might get ahead. However, my father's parents told him they couldn't afford for him to go to school; they needed him to work. He quit school and earned what he could. His sisters also worked. My silent father never told me any of this; it was my mother, who loved him, who told the tales.

When I was very young, my father drove a truck for a tire company. Many years later (he was by then a clerk for the U.S. Postal Service) when I married for a second time, I learned that my new father-in-law had been the vice-president, in those days, of the company for which my father had driven the truck. I remember the two men meeting before the wedding and—less awkwardly than I would have supposed—trading stories about the people and places they had each, from different vantage points, known in common.

The first childhood memory I have is of my father going away to the navy in 1945, toward the very end of World War II, leaving me, at four years old, in the hands of the three women. I have only one other vivid memory of childhood; it's of my father's return from service. The doorbell rang; my mother answered it, dropped what was in her hands, cried out "Milty! Milty!" (my father's name was Milton), and embraced a thin and haggard man I did not recognize at first. The navy, my father said, had taught him to sleep standing up, but he had never learned, having come from a kosher home, to swallow the breakfast eggs cooked in bacon fat, the ham sandwiches prepared for lunch, and the pork chops served for dinner.

My parents, my grandmother, and my aunt were altogether indulgent and kind to me. I was, as I have said, the firstborn son (my brother was born in 1945, around the time—I think it was just before—of my father's return), and every firstborn Jewish son might be the Messiah come at last, so don't mess with *moshiach*! But I experienced their kindness as horribly asphyxiating. Like Memmi, I felt I had no room to breathe. By the time I had been swaddled in enough layers of clothing to resist the cold of a winter afternoon, it was almost twilight, and since the evening chill could be the death of a child, there was little time for me to play outdoors. The arrival of my brother, Edward, should have split their attention; if so, I have no sense of being less fussed over after his birth than I was before.

My people, like Linda Hogan's, were people without privilege. People compensate for that lack in different ways; my family compensated by overprotecting themselves—and me. We dressed too warmly; we ate and worried too much. America, after all, was violent and dangerous; and yet my people—in this case entirely different from African Americans and Native Americans—could not see Americans in general as their enemies, as meaning them harm. Of course there was anti-Semitism in America; of course one might be treated unfairly. But these were taken as isolated cases, the exception rather than the rule. Jews, like all the other white immigrants, had come to America willingly and hopefully. If there were no streets paved with gold, at least there were no pogroms. Our apartments in the Bronx and then in Manhattan had many locks on the doors, but these were only to protect us from common, garden-variety burglars and intruders; at least in New York City, we did not anticipate the arrival of organized, state-sanctioned tormentors. Nonetheless, my grandmother ate her meals rapidly and sometimes standing up, as though she might at any moment have to take flight. The rest of us saw this only as a sad reminder of what had happened to her in the Old World. Pervasive anti-Semitism was the curse of the Old World, not the New. Racism, of course, is the curse of the New World, but my family, though vaguely and generally "liberal" in its sympathies, did not think or speak of such things.

Extended family gatherings, if my fuzzy recollections are at all accurate, were chaotic and noisy—although even at those times my father did not say much—with everyone talking about food, their children, and their neighbors. When such gatherings were at my parents' apartment (this was after we no longer lived with my grandmother and my aunt, after I was five or six years old), I tried to escape to the little room I shared with my younger brother. When they were held elsewhere, I begged to be left at home. In these evasive maneuvers, I pled the demands of scholarship: I had a lot of homework; I had to study. These demands, I had learned, always counted with my family. Who was I? I was what I did. I was a nice Jewish boy who studied and read.

I was a youthful scholar in two kinds of school. From nine to three o'clock each day I attended the public schools of the Lower East Side, staffed mostly, as I now see it, by mildly sadistic, slightly alcoholic "spinsters" (to use a word of the period), abnormals trained in midwestern "normal" schools, middle-aged women shipwrecked in New York as a result of God-knows-what failed voyages. There were the Garrity sisters—I never knew their first names—one a fourth-grade and one a fifth-grade instructor. Both had wavy red hair and very small spectacles. They screamed and shrieked when angered and cackled when pleased. Their breath had a strange smell sometimes, but since my parents drank nothing stronger then cream soda or Doctor Brown's Celray (except for tiny sips of the requisite four cups of Passover wine), I did not recognize the smell as alcohol. I was never in one of the Garritys' classes, and I report my observations of them as a result of my position as a school "monitor," one of the goody-goodies who got to carry messages and paperwork from classroom to classroom in those days of primitive communication.

I did, however, have Miss Berkelhammer as my teacher in the third grade. She wore a wig and when she raged and yelled—this was often— it slipped to the left or right, requiring regular adjustment. The Garritys were known to lose their temper and occasionally slap a student; Miss Berkelhammer hit as a matter of calculated policy. She would call those who displeased her forward to her desk and strike them on the hand with a ruler. I was never hit at home, and the thought of being struck in public caused me to have nightmares. I think it was my typically silent father who actually spoke on this issue, instructing me to inform Miss Berkelhammer that should she seek physically to discipline me, for any blow she dared to give she would receive at least one in return! (Can this be right? from my accepting, nonviolent father?) Of course it never came to that; I was a well-behaved student under ordinary circumstances, and in these circumstances, I was sufficiently terrified as to make sure that I did nothing to attract Miss Berkelhammer's wrath.

From four to five-thirty every day of the week but Shabbat (though there was class on Sunday mornings), I attended Hebrew school: Talmud Torah, in Hebrew; *cheder*, in Yiddish. Here I was to learn to read the Hebrew alphabet and to translate from the Old Testament's five books of Moses in preparation for my bar mitzvah, the initiation into Jewish manhood that occurs on a boy's thirteenth birthday.

The public schoolteachers were mostly women; the Hebrew schoolteachers were mostly men. The former, as I have said, were—at least in my recollection—middle-aged; the latter were elderly. The secular schoolwomen, even in their mild derangement, were neat and clean in a dilapidatedly genteel fashion; the religious schoolmen were slovenly and gross. The felt hats they wore had dark lines of grease above the headbands; I recall stained waistcoats and an unpleasant odor about their breath and their bodies. Perhaps it was a token of the times, but most of the teachers I encountered, women and men, secular and religious, shared a sadistic disposition, which they would have explained as no more than consistent with sound pedagogical practice, "spare the rod and spoil the child." I violently hated Hebrew school—where, as in no other institution of learning I attended, I did very badly.

But I can't deny that I liked public school, even though my experience was often bizarre and more than a little frightening. It should be said that not all the teachers there were of the sort I have described so far. Some few were kind and sane and dedicated: Miss Rosen, Mrs. Riesman, and—not kind but nonetheless clearly benevolent in intention, a person willing to explain with somewhat grim but great patience—Miss Verprovsky. Even with the scariest of teachers, I found the classroom to be a welcome place, where a general respectful silence prevailed and one person spoke at a time, very different from gatherings at home, where people all spoke at once. Shouting and screaming were not permitted in school, and any inclination to sarcasm or name-calling among the students was instantly nipped in the bud. The value of an opinion, it seemed, was not strictly a function of how loudly or repeatedly it was asserted. Apparently there were rational criteria for establishing the authority of one's views. And though people might disagree, disagreement was not necessarily the equivalent of betrayal. In the miserable public schools of the Lower East Side, I became a convert to the Enlightenment. And neither the ethnic, national, and religious appeals from the "provinces" nor the postmodernist appeals from the metropolitan centers have yet managed to urge me to apostasy.

I fled my family for books; I became "The boy who studies and reads"—fiction in English and, later, in French. Born into an earlier generation, Albert Memmi wrote: "Knowledge was the very origin, perhaps, of all the rifts and frustrations that have become apparent in my life. I might have been happier as a Jew of the ghetto, still believing confidently in his God.... But I could only see, in those days, the element of new adventure. . . . I had the whole world to conquer." I might have said, "in those days," much the same thing.

My own flight from kin and traditional religion never did—as it also did not for Memmi—become a temptation to deny that I was Jewish or that

I was working-class. But I had absolutely no sense of the way in which I might form my personal or vocational identities on the basis of Jewishness or a class position.

We Americans have a particularly hard time acknowledging that our "individual" identities or personal "system[s] of beliefs" may not, on consideration, actually be unique to us. For all of my own awareness of how intensely each of us is shaped by culture and history, it still comes as something of a surprise to discover that, after all, I have turned into very much the sort of person T. S. Eliot found detrimental to the cultural and political health of (Christian) nations—into a "free-thinking," cosmopolitan Jew. Although my background is Jewish, I identify myself "as an enlightened universalist who ha[s] transcended both ethnic provincialism and supernatural religion." These rather stuffy, rather old-fashioned words are used by Leonard Glick to describe Franz Boas, that early and very formidable Jewish boy among the Indians. And it is only now, having for more than fifteen years worked with Native American literatures, that I can recognize myself as something of a descendant of Boas, mutatis mutandis.

Boas was a German Jew of middle-class and progressive background; his family apparently remained true to the "principles of 1848," the (failed) revolutionary commitment to the "establishment of an open constitutional society, liberal in social and political orientation, and favorable to the interest of the emerging bourgeoisie." Boas wrote near the end of his life: "My parents had broken through the shackles of dogma. . . . Thus I was spared the struggle against religious dogma that besets the lives of so many young people. . . . My whole outlook upon social life is determined by the question: how can we recognize the shackles that tradition has laid upon us? For when we recognize them, we are also able to break them."

Leonard Glick, from whose article I take these quotations, notes the contradiction between Boas's sense, here, of religion as "dogma" and of tradition as laying "shackles" upon us, and his ethnographic commitment to "patiently recording the details of myths and religious beliefs of people in cultural worlds immensely different from his own. We see him documenting the ineffable uniqueness of other cultures and arguing for the principle, so central to the discipline he established, that every way of life must be not only permitted but encouraged to flourish *on its own terms*." Glick notes that these "traditions" for Boas, however worthy of preserving, were nonetheless taken as "primitive relics, . . . obstacles in the path toward ethical humanism," Boas's specific version of cosmopolitanism. Personally Boas would have been an adherent of *Zivilisation* while professionally he would have been committed to *Kultur*. In the Germany of Boas's time, as Glick points out:

> In contrast to the English-speaking world, which was tending by this time to merge the terms *culture* and *civilization*, in German the latter word (*Zivilisation*) developed distinctive connotations which established it, somewhat surprisingly, as the precise antithesis of *Kultur*. Whereas *Kultur* evoked images of stability, peasantlike simplicity, and adherence to traditions . . . *Zivilisation* came to be equated with modernization, cosmopolitanism, and opportunism.

For late-nineteenth-century Germans, Jews of Boas's class in particular were the pernicious bearers of *Zivilisation*, whereas for Boas, Jews who were identifiably "Jewish" were the pernicious or "primitive" adherents to *Kultur*.

While he maintained a rather untheorized (Boas's aversion to theory is well-known) attachment to his German identity, a specifically Jewish identity for Boas could be responded to only negatively: it provided examples of the sorts of dogmas and traditions that shackled the individual. Lower-class, uneducated, Eastern European Jews—my people, that is, who were identifiably Jewish—were looked down upon by Boas, the middle-class, educated, *German* Jew. And he was less sympathetic to them than he was to the Native Americans he would study as a specialist in *Kultur*/culture.

Boas, Glick notes firmly, "was determined not to be classified as a Jew," even though he was proud to be "classified" as a *German* American. I know and have not forgotten where I come from, and it is a place quite different from Boas's origins. Still, I too don't much care to be "classified" as a Jew, inasmuch as such classifications usually operate as closures, essentialist totalizations: a Jew is a Jew is a Jew or, in Arif Dirlik's phrase, the Other "as an essence without history." But, one way or another, whatever the meaning of the label may be, yes, I am a Jew, and my class origins are much below those of Boas. Nonetheless, my feelings about *Kultur* and *Zivilisation* in many ways resemble his. I think Boas and I would both agree with Lionel Trilling's (rather huffy!) statement, "I should resent it if a critic of my work discovered in it either faults or virtues which he called Jewish." And yet, I must admit that I should not "resent it" at all if critics of my work discovered in it either faults or virtues that they called "working-class."

In Glick's article cited above, Boas went on to say: "The in-group . . . must be expanded to include all humanity. . . . The solidarity of the group is presumably founded on fundamental traits of mankind and will always remain with us. It must be the object of education to make the individual as free as may be of automatic adhesion to the group in which he is born." Boas's reverence for the putatively autonomous individual and his somewhat rigid bourgeois conceptualization of an opposition between the individual and the group or society are surely suspect today. Nonetheless, I can't deny that I share his view that freedom from "automatic adhesion[s]" is a good thing, that "tradition" can and often does "shackle," and that "in-group" moralities that do not find a way to include "all humanity" are likely to produce the horrors that Dalila Suhonjic has lived. So far as we may be called on to choose between *Einheit* (oneness, unity) and *Freiheit* (freedom), I would, with Boas, choose the latter.

In these regards, Boas and I are each "cosmopolitan critic[s] of particularism," and thus, as Tony Judt has written, each of us is "a direct descendant of John Stuart Mill." Judt offers a quotation from Mill worth reproducing in full. Mill wrote:

> Nobody can suppose that it is not more beneficial to a Breton or a Basque . . . to be . . . a member of the French nationality, admitted on equal terms to all the privileges of French citizenship, sharing the advantages of French protection and the dignity and prestige of French power than to sulk on his own rocks, the half-savage relic of past times, revolving in his own little mental orbit, without participation or interest in the general movement of the world.

This reeks, of course, of imperial arrogance in its naive or disingenuously inflated valuation of "the privileges of French"—or British—"citizenship," French or British protection, dignity, and prestige. The Breton or Basque clinging to his own "rocks" may not be sulking but exploiting the resources of an identity that is geocentrically based; he or she may have a *relationship* with those "rocks," a relationship that Mill, Boas, and I cannot very well imagine, let alone know. And any disinterest he or she might have "in the general movement of the world" is more than compensated for by an interest in the movement of the earth, the stars, the seasons, and the animal-persons who live in and around those "rocks." In the same way, the education that Mill and Boas and I would prescribe for the purposes of freeing us of "automatic adhesion to the group" is not the education that the Basques or Bretons would want for their children.

Nor is it what many contemporary Native Americans want for their children. As Cheryl Crazy Bull has written, "Cultural knowledge restoration and preservation is a primary mission of all tribal colleges." Teachers at the tribal colleges, so far as I am aware, teach in a manner consistent with what is taken as the Navajo, or Lakota, or other traditional "way" of the people, the "group" to which they very much want their students to "adhere." The Western ideal of critical rationalism—of instruction, that is, in intellectual methods that might guide one in the attempt to break some of the "shackles" of "tradition"—is as much an abomination as what Cheryl Crazy Bull calls "the separation of spirituality and education." She wrote:

> Regardless of formal religious affiliations, it would be unheard of in our tribal communities and institutions to ban such [spiritual] practices. So when Sinte Gleska University holds its commencement exercises, we have prayers by religious leaders and medicine people, songs by a drum group, and the tying on of eagles [*sic*] feathers and plumes to honor our graduates' achievements. In this way we are engaging in practices forbidden in American education.

> *"Forbidden, sure, but regularly engaged in anyway, as with all those benedictions and prayers preceding the graduation, or maybe the football game. In this regard we are hypocrites!"*

Cheryl Crazy Bull is correct, of course: I read in the *Lakota Times* on May 11, 1994, of an Oglala woman, Denise Abourezk, who transferred out of Stevens High School in Rapid City, South Dakota, because the school refused to allow her and her seven Native American senior classmates to "receive an eagle feather during the June 5 graduation ceremony." The *Lakota Times* reporter viewed the school's action as a racist snub to Native students. I suspect that's exactly what it was, for it's obvious that, as my friend noted just above, Americans regularly violate the principle of church-state separation in the schools.

I think the Stevens High Indian students should have been allowed to receive their eagle feather—

> *"So you're not all that completely an Enlightenment type, since you can live with contradiction, thinking six things in the morning and having to deal with another very different six in the afternoon and evening!"*

—even though I approve wholeheartedly of the separation of church and state, indeed wishing, with Voltaire, for the demise of both churches and states: *Ni Dieu, ni Maître.* My favorite quotation for a long time has been from Voltaire; as I remember it, it goes something like this: "We will never be free until the last king has been strangled with the entrails of the last priest!" But today the list of those lining up to dance on Voltaire's grave grows rapidly.

Voltaire—oh, dear!—and Mill and Boas! Just a bunch of "dead white males" who wrote from imperial, metropolitan locations. But there are others who share their views in one form or another, and not all of them are male, or white, or from the metropolis. Vizenor, for example, although he intentionally writes a prose that resists semantic clarity, *seems* to want a postindian "tribal knowledge" that is rather different from a *return* to dimly known traditional ways.

And there is, as well, Frantz Fanon. In the central chapter of Fanon's *The Wretched of the Earth*, called "The Pitfalls of National Consciousness," Fanon begins by saying, "History teaches us clearly that the battle against colonialism does not run straight away along the lines of nationalism." I understand national consciousness to have some of the same dangers as tribal consciousness, ethnic consciousness, racial consciousness, and the like. Thus national consciousness, as Fanon continues, must "be enriched and deepened by a very rapid transformation into a consciousness of social and political needs, in other words into [real] humanism." It is Edward Said who inserts the word *real* into the citation from Fanon; I have quoted Said quoting Fanon. Said glosses Fanon as follows: "How odd the word 'humanism' sounds in this context, where it is free from the narcissistic individualism, divisiveness, and colonialist egoism of the imperialism that justified the white man's rule."

Indeed, and we have already seen how Kwame Anthony Appiah's recuperation of humanism in the context of Africa also wants to sound "odd" in just these ways. I like to imagine that if Boas were alive today, he would also subscribe to this revisionist humanism, a "real" humanism. And yet, as Memmi points out, Fanon himself apparently "grew impatient, and failed to hide his scorn of regional particularisms, the tenacity of traditions and customs that distinguish cultural and national aspirations." Fanon, Said, and I too may be in the grip of what Memmi has called "a certain amount of revolutionary romanticism." Our utopian impulse to have the "in-group" expanded to include "all humanity" (Boas's words) may be well and good, but as Memmi says, "one doesn't leave one's own self behind as easily as all that"—a self, as I take it, strongly determined by all sorts of "particularisms," colonial or not. So perhaps I and these few I cite are merely succumbing to the myth of freedom from myth.

Meanwhile, it is painfully true, as I noted earlier in recalling Theodor Adorno, that nationalism is obsolete and current everywhere today. In an autobiographical moment even Said, considering Ras Beirut, "the area where the American University [in Lebanon] is located," noted that although until the Civil War it contained "a nonsectarian, pluralistic, and open community of scholars, political activists, business people and artists," nonetheless, "everyone knew what everyone else's religion and sect and ethnic origin were. They were acknowledged almost subliminally . . . but they *were* noted. You registered and heard it registered that Vahe was an Armenian from Smyrna active in Maronite politics, or that Monah was a Sunni intellectual . . . , etc."

So who are you? Who are you really? It's no wonder, as Daniel Bell wrote almost fifty years ago, that the power of nationalism comes from its recapitulation of the authority, sense of identity, and warmth that families offer. Is it only those of us who sought to flee "the family structure" who would deny the logic of *natio-* and nationalisms? Are there no other structural logics available as the glue for a community offering protection, identification, and warmth?

But let me return to me. We last saw me trying to escape the protection and warmth of my family for books of a predominantly Gallic hue, fiction books mostly. I read not to find my own experience validated by representation—though that might have been useful—but instead to find images of what I might be. Books were, as they have remained for me, the first-last-best chance to "know"—vicariously, indirectly, and so on—experiences I have not or could not have. Surely one of the most extraordinary achievements of contemporary Native American writers—initially, for me, Momaday and Silko—is to have represented an experience very distant from mine with such power as to cause me to want to stay with it, to consider it, to examine it, to discover the ways in which aspects of this distant experience could at moments somehow feel very close.

The small apartment in which my parents, my brother, and I lived was in the Jacob Riis Housing Projects, a federally subsidized housing development for low-income veterans and their families. Just south of Jacob Riis was the Lillian Wald development; still further south were the Baruch houses. When asked where I lived, I would not give a building or street address but instead say "the Projects" or, to be more specific, "Jacob Riis." Other project dwellers would say the same, substituting Lillian Wald or Baruch. The Projects were not reservations, of course—to say Jacob Riis or Lillian Wald was not the same as to say Pine Ridge, Fort Peck, or Wind River—but in retrospect, inasmuch as those who lived in the Projects were federally enrolled, low-income survivors of foreign wars and their families, assigned to urban enclaves with very specific boundaries, maybe there is some small way in which the experience of growing up there, just a bit apart from the mainstream, overlaps the experience of Native people from the reservations. The building we lived in—it does have a street address, 108 Avenue D—was thirteen stories high, with something like nine apartments on each floor. We moved there, I believe, in 1946 or 1947, shortly after the development opened.

I didn't know who Jacob Riis was in those days, or Lillian Wald. Baruch seemed to me more nearly a mysterious adjective than a name; there were the Baruch houses, the Baruch gym, the Baruch pool, and in time the Baruch school, part of the City University system. Now I know who these people were, and I'm pleased to have grown up in the Jacob Riis houses, pleased that my life was associated with a memorial to Jacob Riis. I note that outside the new Museum of the American Indian in the old Customs House in New York is a photograph—it's just to the left of the stairs leading up to the entrance—that Jacob Riis took of a Mohawk family in New York. Perhaps if someone had told me, back then, who Jacob Riis was, I might have begun to form my identity around a class position, something that didn't begin to happen until a good deal later. No one told me, and I didn't ask. But, then, my friends and I played basketball in Tomkins Square Park without knowing who Tomkins was, we shopped at S. Klein on the Square—which was Union Square—without knowing whether the square was named for the Northern forces in the Civil War or for organized labor, and we ventured far south to Canal Street, which bore that name for reasons I also didn't know.

After graduating from the oppressive/liberating schools of the Lower East Side, I went to Stuyvesant High School. This was in my neighborhood, more or less, and it was a public school. But it was a selective, or special, school: you had to take a citywide test to get in. Scores were never revealed, so I don't know how well or poorly I did, but I was admitted. Stuyvesant was my first step into a world larger than the Projects. Boys—we were not, then, prematurely hailed as men, nor were any *girls* admitted—from all over the city attended, and it was not so much the relative geographic diversity, with boys from all the neighborhoods of Manhattan and also from the boroughs, as it was the class diversity that startled me. (Racial diversity in those days was minimal, although Stuyvesant today has, I believe, an Asian majority, both men and women.) Some few Stuyvesant boys actually came to school wearing ties and jackets—very few, to be sure, but enough to be visible. A fellow I became moderately close to (he finished second in our graduating class behind someone I never got to know, someone named Hans Christian Andersen) lived in the Columbia University area, on the Upper West Side of Manhattan, and if I remember correctly, I believe he told me that one or both of his parents were psychiatrists.

I had never been north of Forty-Second Street or west of Seventh Avenue. (Columbia is at 116th Street and Broadway, about five miles, give or take, north and west of the Projects, even though distances, in the city I knew at least, were never reckoned in miles.) And when he invited me to come to his place for a visit one weekday or Saturday afternoon, I entered a world I had never known. I had never been in a building with a doorman, a building with a carpeted lobby lined with mirrors and full of sofas and armchairs. Nor could I recall ever having been in an apartment building elevator (office buildings were different) that didn't smell of urine, as those in the Projects always did.

My friends' parents were not at home when we arrived, and I can't say if he had intentionally planned our visit to avoid his parents—either because he felt freer without them around or because he was as concerned about my class origin as I was, until then, more or less oblivious of his. (He was not one of the guys with the ties.) When he opened the door to the apartment, I was overwhelmed. There were large, upholstered chairs and sofas that looked old and that did not have plastic slipcovers over them; on the walls were hung old-looking paintings that clearly had not been chosen specifically to match the colors of the furniture. There were oriental rugs so worn in places that my mother would have been embarrassed to keep them around. And there were bookshelves everywhere. I had never seen so many books outside of a library, had never imagined that so many books could or would be allowed to take up so much wall and floor space in anyone's home.

I don't recall how we spent the afternoon, except that my friend asked if I would like to have a tour of the Columbia University campus nearby. I said I would, and he guided me around. Toward evening, I took the subway back home to the Projects, to our wall-to-wall carpeted and relatively bookless apartment. (My memory here is fairly certain: I recall two bookcases, four feet high by two feet wide, which contained the set of encyclopedias my mother had purchased, one volume a week at the supermarket, and an entirely miscellaneous collection of novels and of nonfiction works on Jewish subjects.) Whatever I may have learned from this unique venture to the Upper West Side and Columbia University, what I felt I could put into practice was quite clear. The year was 1957, and though my decision might have, in the tough, working-class Projects, put my life in jeopardy, what I had to have was white buck shoes and a pair of khaki chino pants with a belt in the back!

I graduated 35th in a class of 635. Stuyvesant then—and, I believe, even more so now—was the kind of place to guarantee one's memory of that sort of thing. I applied to Columbia, Cornell, New York University, and, of course, City College. I desperately wanted to get away from home for college. That meant Cornell—which accepted me but did not give me

enough scholarship money so that (even with a New York State Regents'
Scholarship) I could afford to attend. My parents said they would scrimp
and save and so on and so forth so that I could go to Cornell if I wanted to,
but under those conditions I couldn't bring myself to go. Even Columbia
would have cost a good deal, and so I went to NYU, where I was ranked the
top entering freshman for the class of 1962 and was given very generous
scholarship money, with NYU at that time being much in need of students
who could, as the phrase once was applied to President Gerald Ford (who
couldn't), fart and chew gum at the same time.

> *"There is so much in here that is unremittingly sober, bitter, angry!*
> *What about the things you've loved, the pleasures you've had, the*
> *things you enjoy?"*

Such, at any rate, was my "bitter" and "angry" perception. Perhaps it
was in the summer between my high school graduation and my entrance
into college that issues of class became particularly intense for me. I had
been admitted to Columbia and Cornell, and here I was going to NYU; instead of life in a dormitory away from my family, I would live at home.
My friend from the Upper West Side would spend part of the summer
in Europe with his parents and part on Cape Cod before heading on to
Harvard.

We don't ignore race and gender questions when considering identity
but although we always mention class in passing, nothing much is ever
made of it. Kamau Brathwaite, Edward Said, Gayatri Spivak, Fredric Jameson, James Clifford, and Kwame Anthony Appiah, nephew of the king of
Ghana—to mention only a few critics whom I admire enormously—are
not just Barbadian, Palestinian, South Asian, American, and African but
also upper-middle-class or upper-class. Doesn't this matter at all, in the
ways that race and gender matter? If it doesn't (but I think it *does*), is
the fact that I dwell on it even to this extent only further testimony to an
unresolved *ressentiment*, an indication that the Jewish boy might not, as
some of my friends have warned, be so "nice" after all? But class does
matter: how can you do postcolonial theory, as Arif Dirlik sharply notes,
and not speak of global capitalism? How can you talk about identities and
subject-positions and cultural ideology without the class dimension?

> *"But I think writing this has helped you come to peace a bit more with*
> *yourself and who you are. It's really quite gentle for all its intensity."*

It's only lately that I have begun to see class as having something to
do with my attraction to contemporary Native American writers, many of

whom, like me, came from below. Gerald Vizenor was poor and shunted about as a boy; Betty Louise Bell and Louis Owens, along with Linda Hogan, all came from people without privilege—and then there is Carter Revard, who managed to become a Rhodes Scholar despite growing up without electricity or indoor plumbing. Others include Ralph Salisbury, Diane Glancy, Wendy Rose, and the late Mary Tallmountain, none of whom had a comfortable childhood, as well as Charlotte DeClue, Kim Blaeser, Greg Sarris, and so many others.

> *"When you're at one of these fancy academic conferences or receptions, don't you always expect someone to come up and say, 'Hey, you! Beat it, you don't belong here.' You just wait for them to find you out, to announce what you've known all along, that whatever you've done, whoever you've become, you just aren't ever really going to be one of them."*

That's how I feel—though less acutely than I once did (one of the advantages, I suppose, of getting older). Still, although I too may be wearing a suit among the suits, I nonetheless feel like the kid in the dirty, sweaty T-shirt (see below). But I do not feel like this among my friends, the Indian writers and critics whom I've mentioned. With them—in Santa Fe, for instance, at a conference sponsored by Stanford University, where I was the only nonnative speaker, only one of two nonnatives in attendance—I feel OK.

None of this, I want it to be clear, is intended to call into question the value of anyone's commentary on the basis of his or her class formation. Having claimed that the non-Native has every right to be taken seriously when speaking of the Native, I cannot turn and deny to the privileged the right to be taken seriously when speaking of those without privilege. And as I have said, I have the fullest admiration for critics like Said, Appiah, and others who, for all their privileged origins, have chosen to speak on behalf of those without privilege. But like race and gender, class marks us too.

Unlike my friend headed for Harvard, I spent the summer before college at a five-day-a-week job sweeping up and handling the stockroom of a luncheonette on John Street, in the financial district of New York. Friday evenings were the most humiliating, for my task then was to take the board platforms on which the countermen stood all week out into the street and wash them—as the well-dressed Wall Streeters hurried past, careful not to be spattered by my mop and bucket. Once finished, I would get on the bus back home, acutely aware that the suits were keeping a good distance from me in my soiled jeans and sweaty T-shirt.

In the evenings, after dinner with my brother and my parents, I would "hang out." In the Projects, that meant sitting on the vandalized benches in front of one or another building with one's friends, waiting for the end of daylight when, perhaps, something of interest might happen. Not much happened, of course: several girls might show up, and then the talk would get louder and more boastful; or a fight might break out. We might take a walk to see something unusual in the neighborhood: the remains of a car accident, a building under construction. I did not then know the word *multicultural*, but we were quite a multicultural bunch: Jews, Italians, Irish, Puerto Ricans, and African Americans, the last at that time politely referred to as "Negroes" or "colored people."

The Lower East Side in the 1950s had a moderate amount of gang culture and warfare, and many of the black and Puerto Rican guys I knew were members of gangs, the Sportsmen for the blacks and the Dragons for the Puerto Ricans. (There were Irish and Italian gangs too, but they seemed not to have drawn many members from Jacob Riis. It was only much later that I heard of Jewish gangsters.) Shortly before I graduated from college and left the Projects, I discovered the word "Colegenes" spraypainted on the walls of several of the buildings. This was the name of a new, multiracial gang who called themselves, never mind the spelling, the *Collegians*.

Occasionally on a Friday or Saturday night, my black and Puerto Rican friends would ask some of us white guys to hold—that is, to hide on our bodies or nearby—their weapons, which were very low-tech by today's standards: switchblade knives, brass knuckles, homemade guns called zip guns, an occasional short length of chain, or half a baseball bat. They gave the weapons to us because, on the weekend, the local police would sweep through the Projects and roust males of color between the ages of fourteen and twenty or so, presumably in the interest of preventing gang violence.

All white in that era, the cops would come up to us on the benches and make obscene racist remarks about mothers or sisters in the hope of provoking a response that would justify their beating the shit out of the respondent. The black and Puerto Rican guys were hip to the routine, usually confining themselves to rolling their eyes, shaking their heads, and softly saying, "Oh *man*." But even relative passivity could not prevent the cops from slapping, pushing, shoving, or—just for the fun of it—poking a nightstick into someone's ribs or Adam's apple.

Eventually, the cops would get around to doing a body search of the black and Puerto Rican guys, paying no attention whatever to the rest of us, white guys who either had on us or had right nearby the weapons the cops presumably were seeking to confiscate. The predictably futile search being completed, our heros in blue would depart with some last blow or obscenity. There would be silence until they were *almost* out of earshot, then someone would shout, "motherfuckers!" "assholes!" or *le comble*, which is how I think it is said in French, the ultimate insult in the macho 1950s: "faggits!"

As the night wore on, we white boys were instructed to get the "stuff" for our darker friends. Once armed, they would set out into the night for battles the nature and outcome of which we would learn only later. Occasionally someone did not return, or was arrested, or lost an eye or some fingers. I remember one time going to watch my younger brother's Little League baseball team play on the fields of East River Drive Park and noticing they had no second baseman and no right fielder. "Where are those guys?" I asked him. He said the right fielder had been killed the night before, and the second baseman, so far as they knew, was in "juvie hall," juvenile detention. Little League rules specified that a team must forfeit its game if it could not field the requisite nine players, but rules were bent on the Lower East Side: my brother's team played seven men against nine. I remember that they won, unless this is only an instance of "the distortion of truth by memory," as Boas near the end of his life said of all autobiographical writing.

The Jewish guys usually didn't get killed or arrested (getting beat up was another thing), and most of us, after high school graduation, were headed for college to become accountants, engineers, and in a few cases, even doctors or lawyers. The Italian guys frequently had relatives who would either take them into a family business or—I am very wary of perpetuating stereotypes, yet this was my experience—get them some entry-level mob position. The Irish guys were going to take whatever job they could get or, in several cases, join the Marines. I can see now that it was the Puerto Rican and African American men, "the persons of color," as we currently say, whose path was least clear: they too would look for one job or another; some would also enter the armed services; few, if any, spoke of family who could help them materially in any way. What the young women would do was hazy to me, the 1950s being an age of intense gender separation. Many, I think, went to college, to schools of education or nursing; some got jobs in offices; most, it is my recollection, hoped to marry soon.

When I got to college, the most exciting course my freshman year was not the literature course but a sociology class. (There was no literature course; we all had to take "freshman writing.") I had read Vance Packard's rather silly book about TV and subliminal advertising, *The Hidden Persuaders*. I found it fascinating and began to think about the complementary and oppositional relation between popular culture and high culture—not, of course, that I would or could have put it that way. I thought a course in sociology would tell me about these things, though I was not, to be honest, entirely sure whether I hoped that it would help me to avoid being unduly manipulated or that it would teach me the art of manipulating others.

One reading in our required text had a passage in which the authors announced the wholly objective-sounding proposition that people of working-class background who wanted to advance themselves by means of education would do best to apply themselves to mathematics and the sciences because they could not possibly hope ever to make up for the early exposure to music, art, literature, and travel—to High Culture worldliness—that they had never had and that success in a life devoted to "the humanities" would surely require. I felt this passage speaking to me, and my response was mixed. On the one hand, I had the sinking feeling that the textbook was probably correct, that I—from my home with few books, with no music, paintings, or museum trips, with no visits to the theater or to Europe—could *not* ever catch up to the sons and daughters of Upper West Side psychiatrists and their peers. On the other hand, I had a certain rebellious optimism: the 1950s, after all, *was* an expansive period; it did seem possible to work and get somewhere. Like Memmi long before me and in a faraway place, I too thought "knowledge" might be enough to help me conquer the world.

As the authors of the sociology text knew, however, knowledge alone was not enough. If poor kids could not ever quite catch up to the culturally comfortable, at least they could learn good manners! Some such notion, I suppose, was the premise on which the Jonah Goldstein Foundation had been established, which, toward the end of my senior year in high school, chose me as one of its beneficiaries. The Goldstein Foundation did not give out money for tuition, books, or anything else; rather, it put lowly but promising Jewish aspirants to success in touch with people—*only* Jewish people?—who had already achieved a certain conspicuous success, people willing, on selected occasions, to take a Goldstein grantee under a golden wing. My Goldstein Foundation patron was MHL—I will not identify him further—a graduate of the Wharton School and the founder and CEO of an insurance company called S—— S—— Life, on Fifth Avenue in New York City. I was the blank slate on which he would inscribe the manners and mores of the "Successful Classes."

And so it came to pass that I was, somewhere just past the beginning of my freshman year at NYU, invited to dine with MHL. I go to an Upper West Side apartment building in the eighties or nineties, not much different from (sigh of relief!) my friend's parents' apartment near Columbia:

same doorman, same stuffed furniture in the lobby, same elegant, oldish, clean elevator. MHL greets me at the door. He is a man in, I guess, his early forties: very trim, no coat, dress shirt and tie, suspenders, glass (*martini* glass, I think it was) in hand. "Welcome, welcome, come in, sit down." Huge apartment: large abstract paintings on the walls, no oriental rugs but off-white carpeting.

There is a Mrs. L, younger than MH. Wife number three or four is altogether a more gentle soul than the master, who is given to broad gestures and bursts of loud assertion. "What will you have to drink?" he inquires, adding sans pause: "But of course you don't know what you should drink. That's what we're going to teach you." He gives a slight satisfied chuckle: "heh, heh, heh." Some sort of sweet wine is his choice, maybe a sauterne, maybe some peachy thing, I can't recall, but it is a good choice. Unaccustomed as I am, I sip, not without pleasure. At dinner, the master instructs me in the proper deployment of forks and knives. A black maid serves; MHL notes that I manage well, even with the added handicap of my left-handedness. MHL, at salad time—postmeal, continental style—turns out to be passionate about salad dressing. He makes his own—some standard types, some quite unusual—and he makes them by the gallon. We retire to the living room for coffee. As I take my leave to return to the Projects, I am told that I have done well and will be invited back. I descend into the subway with a quart jar of thick, reddish salad dressing.

I was invited back and was also given summer work—shirt-and-tie work, no more T-shirts—at S—— S—— Life. I was eventually offered— at least I think this is what was proposed by MHL—his daughter's hand in marriage (never mind that, in the few times we had met, his daughter hadn't seemed to like me much) and a fine future in the insurance industry. I said, "Er, um, ah, well . . ." And eventually we lost touch, MHL and me. But along the way he took me to restaurants and the theater, and even though the manner of it was—from my present vantage point, as I could see even then—rather dreadful, patronizing, and militantly insensitive, I did learn a lot. I am very grateful to MHL.

In defiance of my freshman sociology text and with the help of MHL, I took my chance and did not specialize in math or science; instead, I studied literature. I wanted to be a "French major," but because that required courses in French history and geography—and these seemed uninteresting to me—I became a Francophile "English major."

I entered NYU, as I have said, without enthusiasm; I had wanted to leave the ever-narrower-seeming confines of our apartment and the Projects, and I definitely did not want to be a college student still living at home. Nonetheless, I was extremely fortunate at NYU. My first teacher of French was Elaine Marks, later president of the Modern Language Association; when I saw her recently for a brief moment, for the first time in thirty years, she greeted me as "*Monsieur Krupat, mon premier étudiant.*" Marks recently noted that she "began to teach in the 1950s," so that I may not—encountering her for the first time in, I think, 1958—have *literally* been her first student. In any case, it never occurred to me that this brilliant, sophisticated, mature, and to my adolescent eyes, absolutely gorgeous *older woman* (twenty-nine? thirty?) might be a novice teacher. Her "conscious objective," Marks has written, "was to teach anguish, to provoke students into an awareness of their precarious situation in the world."

The young Elaine Marks was an upper-middle-class American Jew and socially secure; her stated attachment to Blaise Pascal and Jean-Paul Sartre was, of course, philosophical. But I was the Jew described in Sartre's *Anti-Semite and Jew*, the socially insecure Jew who had plenty of anguish and plenty of a sense of precariousness well short of the metaphysical horizon. I felt my "precarious situation in the world" most intensely, for example when Miss Marks unexpectedly—miraculously!—invited me to accompany her to the New York opening of Albert Camus's play *Caligula*. I was unsure what to wear. A suit, the tutelage of MHL had made clear, would have been appropriate. But I had only one suit, and it was a bit threadbare and, because I had recently shed some weight, did not fit very well.

Going to our orchestra seats, Miss Marks stopped to introduce me to Mike Nichols, a school or childhood buddy, and said hello in passing (if I remember correctly) to others who were or to me *looked* "famous." I felt, in spades, my precarious situation in *this* world. After Caligula's sister-lover's death, poor Caligula learned that "les hommes meurent, et ils ne sont pas heureux" (men die, and they are not happy)—and learned too that, for all his imperial rank, he could not have the moon. The moon! Ah yes, that would be nice to have, but first, please, how about a new suit that fit?

At NYU, I also studied with Anna Balakian, an important critic of surrealism. One semester, for a French literature survey, my teacher was a man named Georges Borchardt, who was, I was told, Samuel Beckett's literary representative and who is still today, I believe, an active literary agent. M. Borchardt made clear that teaching the likes of us was beneath him, and he treated just about all of us, the good students (*moi*) and the bad, with equivalent contemptuous hauteur. Alas, I loved it.

I also studied with the eminent and awesome and superlatively kind Germaine Brée. In my senior year, she suggested I apply for a Fulbright fellowship to France after graduation. Chip still on shoulder, I said some-thing to the effect that lowly NYU students would not have much of a chance against the Harvard and Yale and Princeton students with whom we would be in competition in the Northeast. She put her hand—familiar gesture by now—through her thick hair already gone gray, smiled very gently, and pointed out that since she was on the Fulbright committee, per-haps an NYU student, a really *good* NYU student, might just possibly have a chance. I asked for Paris; the Fulbright committee in its wisdom sent me to Strasbourg. And so I went to France.

In Strasbourg, I read for the project on the *nouveau roman* that I had proposed to the Fulbright Committee. I studied Latin in a class full of nuns. I listened to a pretentiously Anglomimetic Frenchman lecture on "Wurds-wurt" and "Col-é-reedge." And I discovered that, oddly enough for a Jewish boy from the New York projects, I was deeply American.

This discovery announced itself initially in my first attempt to write a novel. Although I had apparently embarked on what I did not then know was "an academic career," I had been writing fiction in high school and col-lege, and my fondest wish was to be an Artist. I longed to have short fiction appear in the most prestigious periodicals, to publish novel after novel, to be invited to read everywhere in the United States and abroad, and to sleep with as many young women as would succumb to my talent, my presump-tuousness, and my obvious desire. But in fact, in Strasbourg at the age of twenty-one, I was already a married man. Nonetheless, I sat down to write.

What came out—I will not describe it in more detail than this—was a book that was nothing like the French or British fiction I had known (and had imitated earlier). I told a tale in which an older man, some alter-elder ego, set off in a horse and wagon(!) on a cross-country journey, American-continent–wide, to find his son. To prepare myself to write, I reversed Stendhal's practice of reading from the *Code Napoléon* before sitting down to his fictional labors in order that the dry style of the law code might curb his own inherently romantic style. What I did was read passages of William Faulkner before I took up my pen in order that his most-unlawyerly style might fuel my own inherent romanticism. I could not have placed Faulkner in a stylistic tradition of American lyric expansionism from Walt Whitman forward any more than I could have identified or named such a tradition. But, kid from the Projects though I may have been, I knew I wanted that hot Mississippi mud to fill my book!

I was aware of Faulkner because some college friend had recommended *The Sound and the Fury* to me. I had tried to read it on my own the summer of my sophomore year but had given up in a mixture of rage and despair. I would never be smart enough to "get" this book; what a jerk Faulkner was to write so tough. But I eventually tried other Faulkner and found that I could get it, more or less. As for earlier American writers, I knew little more than the names. Then one day in Strasbourg I passed the U.S. Information Service (USIS) library. I walked in and checked out some Herman Melville, some Nathaniel Hawthorne, and some Henry David Thoreau. During my ten months in Strasbourg, I slowed my meticulous rereadings of Alain Robbe-Grillet, stopped doing my Latin homework, and abandoned Willy Wordsworth completely. Instead, I worked on my novel and read as much of the American Renaissance as the USIS library possessed. Just as reading and writing had helped me escape a culture I did not want, so too, in Strasbourg, did reading and writing lead me to a culture I thought I wanted very much: not to French culture, Francophile that I would for some time yet remain, but to American culture. France for me had meant "the world," the furthest horizon a boy from the bounded Projects could see: not merely cloth napkins and an abundance of silverware but also *dry* wines—white, red, and rosé, still and sparkling—instead of cream soda and sweet Manischewitz Concord Grape, High Culture cholesterol—pâtés and croissants and cheeses of every kind—instead of Low Culture cholesterol—chicken soup and fatty brisket, chopped liver, and cream cheese. Only later would I learn that neither France nor Europe was the world. But just then it was not the globe that beckoned; rather it was—amazingly—America that seemed to call me home.

In *French Lessons: A Memoir*, Alice Kaplan asks, "Why do people want to adopt another culture?" She answers, "Because there's something in their own they don't like, that doesn't *name* them." I was drawn to Kaplan's book for obvious reasons: I too am an American Jew who came from a culture I didn't like and who was pulled strongly toward France at one time in my life. But *French Lessons* tells a story very different from mine; the differences may be age-, region-, class-, and gender-based, since Kaplan is at least ten years younger than I, is from the Midwest, is upper-middle-class, and is a woman. And she has had the professional success that my college sociology text promised to people of her class, not to mine. French, as she rather too easily admits, gave her "a place to hide." She concludes her book: "All my life, I've used and abused my gift for language. I'm tempted, down to the last page, to wrap things up too neatly in words." But this is coy and surely self-defeating. She writes that she is tempted, but has she, in these words and the ones that precede them, yielded to the temptation? If she hasn't, why raise the possibility that everything we have read to this point may all be too neat? If she has, doesn't that subvert the ostensible purpose of the book, that is, *not* to wrap things up neatly but in some fashion to work them through? Kaplan hides not only in French but in English as well; her book uses autobiography as a form of intimate evasion. Her efforts with the difficult French "r" are not like Memmi's; there is not the urgency of his "hand-to-hand struggle" with the "r" and the nasals. Maybe class makes the difference—or am I once more being unpleasant by mentioning such a thing? Kaplan's book is in its third printing.

> *"I strongly recommend you excise the attack on Alice Kaplan. It will make an enemy and win no friends."*

Kaplan gets named by leaping over where she came from: her class, her region, "America," the bits of Yiddish in her past. Whether she is hiding or luxuriating, she lives not so much in French culture as in the academic culture of French.

> *"But don't you live in the academic culture of Indians? Surely you don't live in Indian culture."*

I'm grateful not so much to "French" but to France because, as I now examine the matter retrospectively, it did indeed begin to name me. I'm most grateful to France, however, because it made me realize that I would have to go back to America to see what local names I might accept.

I returned to the United States to do graduate work at Columbia University in modern British and American literature, with the two, at that time, still linked for degree purposes. My doctoral dissertation was on several twentieth-century American novelists who were not quite—although the term was not then used—canonical novelists: Nathanael West, Djuna Barnes, Edward Lewis Wallant, and Jack Kerouac. As for Native American literature, none of my teachers in college or graduate school had even remotely hinted that such a thing might exist. Indeed, it wasn't until many years after graduate school—by which time I had divorced, married for a second time, had two young children, and taken a teaching job at Sarah Lawrence College—and to some extent by accident, that I found myself reading D. H. Lawrence's *Studies in Classic American Literature* and William Carlos Williams's *In the American Grain*, both texts of the mid-1920s, and found myself confronting these authors' sense that if you wanted to understand "America," you would have to take into account the original, indigenous, Indian presence on this continent.

Coming to grips with America, it seemed, meant facing the massive fact that the so-called New World was never an uninhabited, uncivilized, wild, and barbarous place, was never "virgin land," in Henry Nash Smith's presently embarrassing phrase, although it was most certainly soon to be—this phrase is Francis Jennings's—"widowed land." I read Williams and Lawrence when, for reasons I can't recall, I was extending my reading in Thoreau. It was a surprise to discover that Thoreau's last words on earth were "moose" and "Indian."

So, belatedly—I was approaching forty and was still so unformed!—it occurred to me that for anyone who wanted to think of himself or herself as "American," the most important names to explore might not be names in English at all but rather names in the native languages of indigenous America. Some of these names were all too familiar—Manhasset, Patchogue, Nantucket, Seneca, Oneida, Sequoia, even Pontiac—although, apart from a large California tree, a large Detroit-made automobile, and some places on Long Island, in New York, and in New England, I had no idea what these names actually named. I knew that Moby Dick had been hunted by a ship call the *Pequod*, but there was nothing, to me, in *that* name.

To think about all this—and also to think about personal and political uneasinesses (this was a difficult time in my second marriage, and Richard Nixon, a hateful and vindictive man, was president.)—I did what I had done for a great many years: I tried to put it all into a novel. I did not then know that narrative was central to traditional Native American cultures, where knowledge of every kind is transmitted in stories. Nor, in choosing to narrate that novel in the plural first person, did I know that traditional Native cultures tended to define the "individual" in communal terms. The book was called *Woodsmen; or, Thoreau and the Indians.*

Woodsmen was the last novel I wrote. After completing it, I began to do what I had never really wanted to do before: to write criticism. But to do that, it became apparent, I would also have to reschool myself, for in the late 1970s, the critical world was at least waist-deep in structuralism, poststructuralism, and a great many other isms for which my generation at Columbia graduate school had been about two minutes too early. So I tried to teach myself about voice and text and sign, all the while avidly reading not Friedrich Nietzsche or Jean-Jacques Rousseau or Plato but N. Scott Momaday, Leslie Marmon Silko, Black Elk, James Welch, and the selections in Frederick W. Turner's *Portable North American Indian Reader.* High theory and low literature—which is, of course, minority, other literature—had not often, so far as I knew, been critically introduced to one another. Might it not, then, be useful for a fuller understanding of Native American literature to examine it using the most high-tech tools available? Might it not be useful as well for the theory to test itself against texts that were, let's say, *unforeseen?* As I embarked on the initial stages of matchmaking (Native literature, meet poststructuralist theory; poststructuralist theory, I'm very pleased to introduce you to Native literature), I was also trying to learn about as many Native cultures as I could.

"So that's what you do, you interpret our culture? You tell folks what's good or bad about these books you write about? Well, what I want to see is whether you're accurate or not."

This approach was, as several have pointed out, Eurocentric. What about indigenous approaches? Recognizing the many Native American perspectives on issues important to criticism today, I have tried to move in what I have several times called an "ethnocritical" direction. But I have not been, nor will I ever be, able to produce a criticism from "an Indian perspective"—nor, as I have argued throughout this book, will anyone else, Native or non-Native, at least not if he or she envisions an indigenous criticism as "sovereign," "autonomous," free from all taint of Europe. Whatever else it means, history means hybridity and the chance— as Vizenor has foremost argued—to invent comic, not tragic, futures. History, as Fredric Jameson has written, *hurts*. Yet for those who survive it, it reveals possibilities for healing too.

I published my first, hesitant critical article on a Native American subject in the *Centennial Review* in 1979, the same year *Woodsmen* appeared. That issue of the *Centennial Review* contained a poem by Brian Swann. Swann wrote me at Sarah Lawrence; we discovered we lived within a few blocks of one another, and we arranged to meet. Swann, a poet, translator, and writer of fiction, had been reading Native literatures for some time, and he also knew the work of the ethnopoetic movement: Jerome Rothenberg, another nice Jewish boy who had been attracted to Indians; Armand Schwerner, ditto; and among others, a nice goyish boy, Dennis Tedlock, an innovative transcriber and translator from the Zuni and, later, the Quiche Maya. I learned a lot from Swann, and our association continues to be important to me.

It was at this time that, for reasons others have documented, autobiography studies began to flourish. Among the selections in Turner's *Indian Reader*, I had been particularly taken with "The Autobiography of a Winnebago Indian," a text produced by the anthropologist Paul Radin—a student of Boas and one more Jewish boy (from a rabbinical family, no less!) among the Indians. What impressed me was this Winnebago man's ability to speak about himself without egotism. The notion that Native American autobiography might hold models for what Paul John Eakin has called the "relational self," a self very different from that of the dominant American 1980s me-ist, was fascinating to discover.

Just as in France I had found America and American literature, in America and American literature—Faulkner, Lawrence's study, Williams, and in particular Thoreau—I began to find Native American literature. Now, reading Native American writers, I am increasingly drawn outward toward a broader world. Whether in the particular contemporary literary context of postcolonialism or in the concern for "culture and imperialism," "difference," "canonization," and "marginalization," I can't help but feel that my desire to listen to such people as Ngũgĩ wa Thiong'o and Buchi Emecheta, to the women in Barbara Harlow's *Barred*, to C. L. R. James, Sara Suleri, and Stuart Hall, to George Lamming and Kamau Brathwaite, and to many others I know too little of helps to contextualize my readings of Native American history and literature while my readings of Native American history and literature serve as contexts for my understanding of these global writers. From the Projects to Paris and back to America, and now—dare I say?—on to the world. So, who am I?

I am not a Navajo, as my friend Pat Hilden assured Harriet Skye. I am not Saint Francis, either, although once my life depended, for a moment, on a certain physical resemblance. Here is an early scene from a career.

My friend the anthropologist Donald Bahr had driven us out to a village on the Tohono O'odham Reservation, about five miles past Why, Arizona. We were going to visit A. C., whom Bahr said had begun to dream some extraordinary songs. We pull up near a cinder-block house and wait. Eventually, A. C. comes out and invites us in. It is a Sunday afternoon; he's been to church, had lunch and a couple of beers. He talks quietly to Bahr in Papago. Bahr says, "Uh-oh, much stuff about owls, powerful stuff"; I'm not sure what this all means. We enter. A. C. invites us to the kitchen table, offers some fruit, and chides Bahr for not bringing something nice to drink. He persuades us, finally, to drive just off the reservation to get some sweet wine, being very specific as to what he wants. We go. The store is out of the wine, so we get the nearest thing to it we can find. We return, sit; then we all drink. A. C. jumps up, comes back with a couple of owl feathers, talks some more to Bahr in Papago, then sits back down at the table.

Bahr asks A. C. if he feels like singing any of his songs. Bahr tells him that I have come a very long way to hear him sing. "From where?" A. C. asks. Perversely Bahr says, "From France." A. C. isn't sure just where that is but says he has heard it's a nice place. Before he will sing, he wants us to sing. Bahr sings several Pima songs. A. C. is pleased. He jumps up again, quickly comes back without a word, but shakes his head now. He insists I should sing. I say I can't sing, don't know how, don't know any songs. "Sing songs from your country," A. C. insists. "*Sing!*" I actually manage a few verses of a French song I learned my first time in Paris. A. C. says it's a good song, he likes to hear it. "But what does it mean?" Bahr, consistently perverse, offers a bawdy story as translation for my sentimental song about spring and lost love. A. C. is amused, pats my shoulder, and launches into Papago, using English to name sexual parts and acts. Bahr laughs but looks disturbed and gets up, saying maybe we should go.

"No!" A. C. insists: he hasn't sung yet. We sit down. He picks up a very large knife from the kitchen table and begins to chuckle. "Maybe I sing," he says, "or maybe I kill you, huh?" He speaks in Papago. "The owls," Bahr says, "very dangerous." "Yes," A. C. continues, headed toward me with the knife, "maybe that's what, I should kill you." Bahr is a large man, and A. C., like me, is not very big at all. I sit, moderately terrified, assuming that Bahr will say or eventually do something to prevent my being killed. A. C. is clearly not sure what he wants to do. He comes close to me, then suddenly throws down the knife and crosses himself. "Dios mío," he says, "ay! San Francisco!" He points my way, crossing himself again and gesturing with his head to the wall behind me.

I turn and see a black-and-white drawing of Saint Francis. The saint, in the picture, has a face shaped approximately like mine and a beard of roughly the same shape as mine. A. C. sits down at the table, shakes his head, and mumbles some sort of apology. He and Bahr talk softly for a while in Papago. It's all because of the owls. We rise, take our leave, and drive off toward Phoenix. Bahr plays a very brief tape he has made of A. C. singing. The sound is poor, the volume close to inaudible. Bahr nods his head appreciatively. This is my first time among the Indians. I'm not from France, and I'm not Saint Francis either. Who am I?

I continue to believe that who I am is largely what I do. What I do is teach, speak, and write about American culture with a particular emphasis on Native American literature. The culture that names me, however, is not so much the many cultures of America or any specific Native American culture. Rather, the culture that best names me is the transnational or cosmopolitan culture of criticism whose "social goals," as Edward Said has written, "are noncoercive knowledge produced in the interests of human freedom." Boas, I imagine, probably thought that this was the kind of criticism he was engaged in producing; so too thought Claude Lévi-Strauss, who in 1942 was in New York, at Boas's side when Boas died. Vizenor too, like his creations Laundry and Stone Columbus, works in the interest of a universal tribe, his writing devoted to healing, "no blood attached or scratched." The tribes are dead; long live tribal values.

Said and Boas were obliged by unfortunate circumstances to leave the parts of the world in which they were first formed. Likewise Simon Ortiz does not live at Acoma now, although Acoma, he often says, is with him wherever he goes. Vizenor too lives far from Minneapolis and the White Earth Reservation, and other Native American writers—Louis Owens in New Mexico, Betty Bell and Bill Penn in Michigan, Linda Hogan in Colorado, Carroll Arnett and Diane Glancy in Minnesota, among others— have also found places for themselves far from their places of origin. Do some of these Native writers, with their strong sense of home, participate in what Said, the displaced Palestinian, calls "exilic consciousness," a particularly useful consciousness, Said argues, for the critic? And what about me? For years I have lived less than a mile from the Jacob Riis Housing Projects where I grew up. Can I be at home in a cosmopolitan culture of criticism while still, as it were, at home?

In a discussion of Erich Auerbach—who, a Jewish refugee from the Nazis, wrote his greatest book in Istanbul during World War II—Said first quotes Auerbach's comment that "our philological home is the earth: it can no longer be the nation" and next cites Auerbach's quotation of Hugh of St. Victor: "He to whom every soil is as his native one is already strong; but he is perfect to whom the entire world is as a foreign land." Or, as Said gives the Latin original, *perfectus vero cui mundus totus exilium est,* which I roughly construe as follows: "He is truly perfect to whom the entire world is his exile." The rest of the passage from Hugh confirms that the "perfect man has extinguished his" love of all places. This "exilic credo" of "willed homelessness," according to Auerbach, "is a good way also for one who wishes to earn a proper love for the world"—not, I think, what Hugh of St. Victor, his sights fixed on heaven, had in mind.

Yet for all my intellectual attraction to notions of this kind, the idea of a "willed homelessness" feels perverse or masochistic to me. Doesn't everyone want some place to call "home"? Maybe somewhere between the longing for rootedness and the choice of exile is the condition theorized by many today as that of *diaspora,* theorized by Daniel Boyarin and Jonathan Boyarin—antagonists, in the past, for Said—as "a theoretical and historical model to replace national self-determination" and to replace, as well, an "uncritical valorization of indigenousness (and particularly the confusion between political indigenousness and mystified autochthony)." The Boyarins note that whatever the historical causes of diaspora, it has for many Jews long been a chosen condition, "the majority of Jews liv[ing] voluntarily outside of the Land." Is this true as well not only for Native American artists and intellectuals in Berkeley, Albuquerque, Ann Arbor, or Boulder but also for Native people in Los Angeles, Minneapolis, and elsewhere? Do they too, like the Jews of whom the Boyarins speak, have "an ability to detach loyalty from place while retaining memory of place"?

The most usual definitions of *diaspora*, as James Clifford has noted, define it "against 1) norms of nation-states and 2) indigenous and especially autochthonous claims by 'tribal' peoples." But Clifford also notes that the tribal-diasporic division is not absolute. Yet diaspora or—to return to Said—exilic consciousness may well be the necessary condition for the cosmopolitan critic today. Meditating further on place and placelessness, Said chooses "the word *culture* to suggest an environment, process, and hegemony in which individuals and their works are embedded." For him, "It is in culture that we can seek out the range of meanings and ideas conveyed by the phrases *belonging to* or *in* a place, being *at home in a place*."

For me, as I have said, this means the culture of criticism; it is the culture of criticism that is increasingly my home. Criticism is what I do, who I am, where I most intensely live. As an American Jew who supports Israel (as I support the United States or any other nation-state) only when it does not engage in imperial adventures and the further oppression of those without power, as one who takes the Jewish diaspora as a historical fact and a potential model for cosmopolitan existence, as a "native" New Yorker fed up with the Big Shitty, my chief sense of "belonging to or in a place, being at home in a place," comes from the culture of criticism.

But my criticism focuses on the cultural production of Native Americans, and all the accounts from Indians today—I know of no alternative discourse with the exception of moments in Vizenor's writing—insist on a geocentrism that borders on autochthony.

> *"Well, sure, but what about the great Athapaskan migration to the Southwest and to California from Alaska/Northwest Canada? In other words, there is a continuous history of mobility for many Native peoples that belies a universal attachment to place. It is amazing how quickly, for example, Navajos have established new place attachments in areas they have only recently appropriated from Hopis, and 'forget' the places they have moved in from."*

This is true enough, but this is not the party line.

As a critic of Native American literatures, I live some of the same contradictions as Boas, who wanted, on the one hand, to transcend the "shackles" of "automatic adhesions" and traditions while, on the other, to record meticulously—and indeed in most appreciative fashion—the work-ings of tradition. I have said that I think of myself as a (grand)child of the Enlightenment. But I am well aware of what Clifford has called "the com-plicity of rationality and terror," of rationalization as economization, of the horrors resulting from the universalization of "the rights of man," as Etienne Balibar has written, in the form of an imperial commitment "to educate the human race."

So I send money to the tribal colleges while believing in the separation of church and state; I support the Lakotas and other indigenous peoples in their efforts to obtain political sovereignty and cultural integrity while I remain wary of all forms of mystified autochthony and willed isolation—of claims, in a conjunctural world, to "autonomy." As a dweller in criticism, I live the perhaps inevitable contradictions of what Gayatri Spivak has called the poststructuralist predicament of criticizing a system that one cannot help but intimately inhabit. I have called for an *ethnocriticism*, a cross-cultural, cross-blood (in Vizenor's term) criticism, while my own practice is (inevitably) deeply embedded in the Western episteme.

Thus I wonder at times whether my position isn't rather like the hope-less position of "the leftist colonizer," as described by Memmi, one for whom "being on the left means not only accepting and assisting the na-tional liberation of the peoples, but also includes political democracy and freedom, economic democracy and justice, rejection of racist xenophobia and universality, material and spiritual progress. Because such aspirations mean all those things, every true leftist must support the national aspira-tions of peoples." Yet, as Memmi continues, there comes a point when the leftist "discovers that there is no connection between the liberation of the colonized and the application of a leftwing program. And that, in fact, he is perhaps aiding the birth of a social order in which there is no room for a leftist as such, at least in the near future."

Memmi pursues his tough-minded and unsentimental analysis, noting that because they are "oppressed as a group, the colonized must neces-sarily adopt a national and ethnic form of liberation from which he [the leftist] cannot but be excluded." In the end, the leftist's "only choice is not between good and evil, but between evil and uneasiness." In the cur-rent climate of Native American studies, the non-Native critic cannot but begin to feel a certain uneasiness. Memmi sees no solution other than for the left colonizer—in this instance, the member of the dominant culture who wants to support subordinated cultures—to deliver himself to the metropolis. What would this mean for me? Would it mean to write about

Joseph Conrad and Emily Brontë, as I did once, long ago? This is valuable work but is not the work that now names me.

I think, then, that there is nothing to do but to try to tolerate the uneasiness and—as Arthur Koestler's Comrade Rubashov put it in *Darkness at Noon*—to try to be useful without vanity. Nonetheless, to cite Memmi once more, "there are . . . impossible historical situations," and who knows, maybe for me, as for the "left colonizer," this is one of them.

Who am I? Do my family beginnings—Russian Jewish immigrant, working-class, New York—explain in any measure my ends, my "identity" as a cultural critic of Native American literatures? It would appear that things just might work the other way around. My grandfather was killed for being a Jew just as Native Americans were killed for being what they were; my grandmother, early an influence on my life, was a person of oral culture; I grew up in a bounded enclave, the Projects, which has some distant and minimal relation to reservation experience. Yet not even in retrospect, when the impulse to produce causes for effects is particularly acute, does this go very far in explaining why I do what I do.

Rather than my origins explaining my ends, my ends, it seems, have forced me to consider my origins. I think here of a passage in Frantz Fanon's *Black Skin, White Masks*, in which he quotes his reception by a white child: "Mama, see the Negro! I'm frightened." Fanon wrote, "I wanted to be a man, nothing but a man." But others will not allow that—ask Dalila Suhonjic, who just wanted to be a Bosnian. Who are you? The othering gaze answers, "You are a black man, a Jew, a Muslim, a Croat, or a Druse."

In the past couple of years I have begun to feel—so far, only a little—this othering gaze, as some Native people (not all, as yet not even many) look at me and say: "See! There is someone who is not one of us!" It is not that I ever claimed, "wannabe" fashion, to be "one of" the Indians; rather, like Fanon, "I wanted to be a man, nothing but a man," one of the two-leggeds of the earth. But now that I am "other" for some, now that I have experienced (an as-yet-rare experience for white men in the United States) being the negative or opposite of something rather than the unquestioned positive norm, I find myself pressed to consider the *particulars* of who I am.

This is not to retract what I have said over and again: that, whatever my particular background, I am, most of all, what I do. The young Lionel Trilling said of himself, " 'I cannot discover anything in my professional intellectual life' traceable to a specifically Jewish background." I could likewise, now that I am not so young, say this for myself.

"But you are a Jew without Judaism, a purely cultural *Jew? What is that? A matter of bagels and bitter jokes?"*

Although I don't find that my "Jewish background" has specifically affected "my professional intellectual life," I think more and more that my class background has.

This chapter is made up of autobiographical reflections, but I feel no more comfortable than most Native Americans do with me-me-me. Like most Native people, I can best think about my*self* in relation to community, although as I have now said many times, my community is a chosen, consensual, affiliative one—modern, rationalist, secular, diasporic, transnational, and cosmopolitan rather than a community of birth, blood, religion, nationality, and the like.

What may well be paradoxical, however, is the fact that it is exactly such community that American *Jews* in this century have very often chosen. That is, my "individual" or "unique" ambiguity about my Jewish identity is not unique at all; rather, it is a historically identifiable trait of many American Jewish intellectuals, at least from Boas forward.

For when "Jewish immigrants and their children," as David Hollinger has written, "responded avidly to classics of American literature, this response was part of a larger discovery of modern and Western culture generally. . . . Memoirs of intellectual life on the Lower East Side establish beyond doubt that newly liberated Jews grasped simultaneously for Marx and Horatio Alger, George Eliot and Washington Irving, Voltaire and Benjamin Franklin."

Voltaire, do I hear? This tendency of the 1920s, 1930s, and 1940s on the part of the children of immigrants must somehow have found its way to the room I shared with my brother in our little apartment in the Projects. Had I not gone off to France and the usis library, had I simply stayed at home and read, maybe it would have worked out just the same (but then again, maybe not).

C. L. R. James has been much quoted as reminding us that individual persons make history—but only such history as it is possible in their time and place to make. I mention James's astute observation in relation to the quotation above. That is, although it is easy for me to imagine that reading American literature in the 1920s, 1930s, 1940s—even in the 1950s and 1960s, my time—could have been the high road for the sons and daughters of Jewish immigrants to "modern and Western culture generally," I don't think it could have opened to them the literary worlds of African American and Native American people. By the 1920s the texts were there:

Frederick Douglass, W. E. B. Du Bois, James Weldon Johnson, Charles Chesnutt, and Jean Toomer; Eastman, Bonnin, Standing Bear, Mourning Dove, and the poetic translations in George Cronyn's *The Path on the Rainbow* (1918). But these, if they had been noticed—and the only Jew I am aware of who noticed them was Louis Untermeyer—would doubtless have seemed provincial, parochial, limited. (Untermeyer, although he later changed his mind, initially responded to them exactly in this way.) And reading American literature most certainly could not have opened to Jewish sons and daughters the possibilities of exploring what was not Western, was not strictly modern.

But now it is possible—my own trajectory is an illustration of the possibility—for the sons and daughters of immigrant Jews to read American literature *first* as a means of expanding their horizons to modernity and the West, *then* of (not contracting but) *localizing* and focusing on the Native American and African American components of American history and culture without which the United States simply cannot be understood and, ultimately, of making whatever efforts they can to read the world.

I am aware that this may seem grandiose, especially in our time of ethnic-nationalist hunkering-down. But of course, if one does not want to repeat *le trahison des clercs*, then it is incumbent on intellectuals and culture-workers not to take the real as rational (Herbert Marcuse's phrase) but to speak for a "rationality" not currently operative. For myself, I intend to continue to study Native American literatures, for all that I most certainly want to read more of the world.

As I work to a conclusion for this chapter—it could, but I think it should not, go on and on and on—it seems to me that I have adopted a comic structure—a result of Vizenor's influence, maybe, or some deep need of my own temperament. I don't, of course, mean that I've been or have tried to be funny; rather, I've constructed a narrative that moves upward toward integrative possibilities. I want still to be defined by the culture of criticism and to believe that criticism can have not only worldly implications but also, occasionally if indirectly, worldly effects.

This is, then, a comic narrative, yes. But as I prepare this chapter for publication, the killing goes on in Bosnia, bombs explode in Paris and the West Bank, and the New York neighborhoods in which I am most at home have a homeless population density higher than the overall population density of at least five western states. Last June, as I was completing my rough first draft, my daughter was randomly and gratuitously assaulted on the street; forty-four stitches in the emergency room of St. Vincent's Hospital were required for her wounds. And I still call this chapter comic?

At Beth Israel Hospital, just around the corner from where I live, Menachem Schneerson, who was the Grand Rebbe of the Lubavitch Chasidim in New York and was thought to be the Messiah and thus immortal, died in the summer of 1994. He had no children and left no guidelines for the choice of his successor; even today, over a year later (in the fall of 1995), I believe the job remains open. A day or so after Schneerson's death, the *New York Times* announced that Ben Cohen, of Ben and Jerry's Ice Cream, had resigned his position as CEO. Is that post still open as well? If my historical position as a non-Native critic of Native American literatures is "impossible," should I aspire to those positions?

Of course not. My position may be uneasy, but it is far, I think, from impossible. So long as I feel that I can be useful without vanity, I hope to go on being what I have become, someone who reads and writes about Native American literatures, a nice Jewish boy among the Indians.

Notes

88. "believe in this." Dalila published her reflections as "A Plea from a Bosnian Student" in the summer of 1994. The quotation is from page 16 of her text. She had told me that her father was a doctor who worked as part of a team seeking to aid rape victims of the Christian Serbs. I have not seen her at the college this year, and I don't know where she is.

89. universal consumer. My essay "For Multiculturalism" is the conclusion to *Ethnocriticism*. I have indicated a somewhat more wary attitude toward multiculturalism in the introduction, although, as here, I remain "for" it.

89. "ethnic conflict." Dirlik, "Postcolonial Aura," 347.

89. what they write about. The Canadian case is described at the beginning of Linda Alcoff's "On the Problem of Speaking for Others."

90. "conveys that belief." Ortiz, *Woven Stone*, 7, 6.

90. "would do later." Ortiz, *Woven Stone*, 6.

92. "all were killed." These words came to me in a letter from Riva Charmach, my father's first cousin, who today lives in Riga, Latvia. I was unaware of her existence until she wrote to me a little over a year ago.

94. "not good enough." Hogan, "The Two Lives," 237. Ron Paquin's recent autobiography, *Not First in Nobody's Heart*, as its title makes clear, documents the most dire consequences of a life without privilege, as does Anthony Apakark Thrasher's *Skid Row . . . Eskimo*, among many others. Nevertheless, the point needs to be repeated that not all Native Americans' lives are best read as stories of victimization.

96. Greg Sarris. See Sarris's *Keeping Slug Woman Alive*.

97. "overcame me at home." See Memmi's autobiographical novel *Pillar of Salt*, 62–63.

101. "world to conquer." *Pillar of Salt*, 83.

102. "supernatural religion." See Glick, "Types," 546, 547.

102. "break them." Glick, "Types," 555, 560.

103. "modernization, cosmopolitanism, and opportunism." Glick, "Types," 549, 554.

103. called "working-class." Dirlik, "Postcolonial Aura," 334. Trilling is quoted in Hollinger, "Ethnic Diversity," 66.

104. "he is born." Boas is quoted in Glick, "Types," 555.

104. "general movement of the world." The lengthy quotation from Mill is in Judt, "New Old Nationalism," 44–45.

105. "American education." Cheryl Crazy Bull, "Who Should Pass Judgment?," 26.

105. separation in the schools. In the *Lakota Times*, May 11, 1994, p. 26. Abourezk's story appears on pages B1 and B3 of the *Lakota Times* for May 11, 1994.

106. "white man's rule." Fanon, *Wretched of the Earth*, 148. Said, *Culture and Imperialism*, 269.

106. freedom from myth. Memmi is quoted in Henry Louis Gates Jr.'s "Critical Fanonism," 468, and, below, 469.

107. "intellectual . . . etc." Said, *After the Last Sky*, 173.

107. Baruch houses. Jacob Riis (1849–1914) came to the United States from Denmark and found work as a journalist covering the immigrant districts of New York, in particular, the Lower East Side. His photographs and commentaries for *How the Other Half Lives* (1890) brought him to national attention. Lillian Wald (1867–1940) studied nursing and attended medical school, leaving to establish a public health center. By 1913, her Henry Street Visiting Nurses employed ninety-two nurses making two hundred thousand visits annually among the poor. Bernard M. Baruch (1870–1965) became a millionaire by the age of thirty thanks to successful speculation on Wall Street, and he went on to advise Presidents Woodrow Wilson, Warren Harding, and Herbert Hoover, among others. His proposal to the United Nations in 1946 for international control of atomic energy was vetoed by the Soviet Union in the Security Council.

108. reasons I also didn't know. Canal Street was named for the canal dug in 1805 to drain the Collect (a freshwater pond polluted by tanneries and soap- and candle-making establishments) into the Hudson River. But the canal bred mosquitoes and was filled in within the decade; the bridge that had spanned it at Broadway was buried and incorporated into the roadway. Tomkins Square was named for Daniel D. Tomkins, four-term governor of New York State and initiator of the law that would abolish slavery in New York on July 4, 1827, two years after his death. Union Square was originally called Union Place in 1808 because of its position as the crossing point for many of the city's streets and roads. It was renamed Union Square in 1832, and in the twentieth century it served as a location for many union activities.

112. the *Collegians*. Mario Maffi's recent book *The Lower East Side* has a wealth of information not only about the gang life of the period but also about matters that I either little knew or was unaware of entirely.

113. all autobiographical writing. See Boas, "Recent Anthropology II," 335.

116. "situation in the world." In Marks "Presidential Address, 1993," 370.

118. "adopt another culture." Kaplan, *French Lessons*, 209.

119. the "r" and the nasals. Kaplan, *French Lessons*, 216. Memmi, *Pillar of Salt*, 108.

120. "widowed land." See Smith's *Virgin Land*.

120. *Thoreau and the Indians*. *Woodsmen* was self-published with the help of Cynthia Krupat, to whom I was then married. She designed the book and saw it through the practical aspects of the publishing process, although neither of us knew how to get the book distributed or reviewed.

121. important to me. Swann and I have worked together on a number of projects and continue to be friends and collaborators as Series Editors for *Studies in Native American Literatures*, a series published by the Smithsonian Institution Press.

122. fascinating to discover. See Eakin's recent *Touching the World*.

122. what this all means. Among the Akimel O'odham (Pima) and Tohono O'odham (Papago), as well as other Yuman "dream culture" peoples, owls are harbingers of death.

123. "interests of human freedom." Said, *The World, the Text, and the Critic*, 7.

124. had in mind. Said's quotation of Auerbach and Hugh of St. Victor are also from *The World, the Text, and the Critic*, 7.

125. "memory of place"? From Boyarin and Boyarin, "Diaspora: Generational Ground of Jewish Identity," 711, 715, 718–19, 722.

125. division is not absolute. James Clifford is quoted from his "Diasporas," 307.

125. "at home in a place." Said, *The World, The Text, and The Critic*, 8.

126. "to educate the human race." Clifford, "Diasporas," 317. Balibar is quoted by Boyarin and Boyarin, 707.

126. intimately inhabit. See Spivak's "The Making of Americans: The Teaching of English and the Future of Culture Studies."

126. "in the near future." Memmi, *The Colonizer and the Colonized*, 34 (both quotations).

126. "between evil and uneasiness." Memmi, *The Colonizer and the Colonized*, 39, 43.

127. this is one of them. Memmi, *The Colonizer and the Colonized*, 39.

127. "nothing but a man." Fanon, *Black Skin, White Masks*, 112–13.

127. "specifically Jewish background." Trilling is quoted in Hollinger, "Ethnic Diversity," 66.

128. "Voltaire and Benjamin Franklin." Hollinger, "Ethnic Diversity," 62.

129. read more of the world. The French phrase is, of course, a reference to the important study of that name written by Julien Benda in 1927. See White's *Metahistory*.

130. the summer of 1994. There were a great many police on duty outside Beth Israel Hospital during Schneerson's last illness. On a couple of occasions I saw cops put quarters in the meters where the Lubavitchers' huge "Mitzvah Mobile" was parked—thanks, no doubt, from Mayor Rudy Giuliani to the Chasidim for their support in the recent mayoral election and a clear violation, among other things, of the constitutional separation of church and state.

Works Cited

Achebe, Chinua. *Hopes and Impediments: Selected Essays.* New York: Doubleday, 1989.

Alcoff, Linda. "On the Problem of Speaking for Others." *Cultural Critique* 20 (1991–92): 5–32.

Alexie, Sherman. "The Unauthorized Autobiography of Me." In *Everything Matters: Autobiographical Essays by Native American Writers,* ed. Arnold Krupat and Brian Swann. New York: Random House, 1998.

American Council on Education. *Summary Report 1990: Doctorate Recipients from United States Universities.* Washington DC: Government Printing Office, 1993.

Appiah, Kwame Anthony. *In My Father's House: Africa in the Philosophy of Culture.* New York: Oxford University Press, 1992.

———. "Race." In *Critical Terms for Literary Study,* ed. Frank Lentricchia and Thomas McLaughlin, 274–87. Chicago: University of Chicago Press, 1990.

Asad, Talal. "The Concept of Cultural Translation in British Social Anthropology." In Clifford and Marcus, 141–64.

Asad, Talal, and John Dixon. "Translating Europe's Others." In *Europe and Its Others: Proceedings of the Essex Sociology of Literature Conference,* vol. 1, ed. Francis Barker, Peter Hulme, Margaret Iversen, and Diana Loxley. Colchester UK: University of Essex Press, 1985.

Ashcroft, Bill, Gareth Griffiths, and Helen Tiffin. *The Empire Writes Back: Theory and Practice in Post-Colonial Literatures.* London: Routledge, 1989.

Bahr, Donald. "Whatever Happened to Mythology?" *Wicazo Sa Review* 9 (1993): 44–49.

Bakhtin, M. M. *Speech Genres and Other Late Essays.* Trans. Vern W. McGee, ed. Caryl Emerson and Michael Holquist. Austin: University of Texas Press, 1986.

Bal, Mieke. "First Person, Second Person, Same Person: Narrative as Epistemology." *New Literary History* 21 (1993): 293–320.

Basso, Keith. *Portraits of the "Whiteman": Linguistic Play and Cultural Symbols among the Western Apache*. New York: Cambridge University Press, 1979.

———. " 'Stalking with Stories': Names, Places, and Moral Narratives among the Western Apache." *Cultural Anthropology* (1984): 19–54.

Bell, Betty Louise. *Faces in the Moon*. Norman: University of Oklahoma Press, 1994.

Benda, Julien. *The Treason of the Intellectuals*. New York: Norton, 1969 [1928]

Benjamin, Walter. "The Task of the Translator." In *Illuminations*, ed. Hannah Arendt, trans. Harry Zohn. New York: Schocken Books, 1969 [1955].

Bevis, William. "Native American Novels: Homing In." In *Recovering the Word: Essays on Native American Literature*, ed. Brian Swann and Arnold Krupat, 580–620. Berkeley: University of California Press, 1987.

Blaeser, Kimberley, M. *Gerald Vizenor: Writing in the Oral Tradition*. Norman: University of Oklahoma Press, in press.

Boas, Frank. "Recent Anthropology II." *Science* 98 (October 15, 1943): 334–37.

Boyarin, Daniel, and Jonathan Boyarin. "Diaspora: Generational Ground of Jewish Identity." *Critical Inquiry* 19 (1993): 693–725.

Brathwaite, Kamau. *Barabajian Poems*. Kingston: Savacou North, 1994.

Bright, William. *The Coyote Reader*. Berkeley: University of California Press, 1994.

Brightman, Robert. ĀCAÔÔHKĪ WINA *and* ĀCIMŌWINA: *Traditional Narratives of the Rock Cree Indians*. Hull, Quebec: Canadian Museum of Civilization, 1989.

Carter, Deborah J., and Reginald Wilson. *Minorities in Higher Education*. Washington DC: American Council on Education, 1994.

Castro, Michael. *Interpreting the Indian: Twentieth-Century Poets and the Native American*. Albuquerque: University of New Mexico Press, 1983.

Césaire, Aimé, *Une Tempête*. Paris: Editions du Seuil, 1969.

Charlot, Martine. *Les Jeunes Vergiliens en France*. Paris: CIEM, 1981.

Cheyfitz, Eric. *The Poetics of Imperialism: Translation and Colonization from "The Tempest" to "Tarzan."* New York: Oxford University Press, 1991.

Churchill, Ward. *Fantasies of the Master Race: Literature, Cinema, and the Colonization of American Indians*. Ed. M. Annette Jaimes. Monroe ME: Common Courage Press, 1992.

Clausen, Jan. "The Axis of Herstory: Review." *Nation* 258 (May 18, 1994): 634–36.

Clifford, James. "Diasporas." *Cultural Anthropology* 9 (1994): 302–38.

———. *The Predicament of Culture: Twentieth-Century Ethnography, Literature, and Art*. Cambridge: Harvard University Press, 1988.

Clifford, James, and George Marcus, eds. *Writing Culture: The Poetics and Politics of Ethnography*. Berkeley: University of California Press, 1986.

Coiner, Constance. "Introduction: Working Class Studies." *Radical Teacher* 46 (1995): 2–4.

Cook-Lynn, Elizabeth. "Cosmopolitanism, Nationalism, the Third World, and Tribal Sovereignty." *Wicazo Sa Review* 9 (1993): 26–36.

———. "The Radical Conscience in Native American Studies." *Wicazo Sa Review* 7 (1991): 9–13.

———. "Who Gets to Tell the Stories?" *Wicazo Sa Review* 9 (1993): 60–63.

Crazy Bull, Cheryl. "Who Should Pass Judgment?" *Tribal College* 5 (1994): 25–28.

Cruikshank, Julie. *Life Lived Like a Story: Life Stories of Three Yukon Native Elders.* Lincoln: University of Nebraska Press, 1990.

DeLoria, Vine, Jr. *God Is Red.* New York: Grosset and Dunlap, 1973.

DeLoria, Vine, Jr., and Clifford Lytle. *The Nations Within: The Past and Future of American Indian Sovereignty.* New York: Pantheon, 1984.

Digest of Education Statistics, 1990. Washington DC: National Center for Education Statistics, 1990.

Dirlik, Arif. "The Postcolonial Aura: Third World Criticism in the Age of Global Capitalism." *Critical Inquiry* 20 (1994): 328–56.

Drinnon, Richard. *Facing West: The Metaphysics of Indian-Hating and Empire-Building.* Minneapolis: University of Minnesota Press, 1980.

Ducrot, Oswald, and Tzvetan Todorov. *Encyclopedic Dictionary of the Sciences of Language.* Trans. Catherine Porter. Baltimore: Johns Hopkins University Press, 1979.

Durham, Jimmie. "Cowboys and . . . Notes on Art, Literature, and American Indians in the Modern American Mind." In Jaimes, *Native America*, 423–38.

Eakin, Paul John. *Touching the World: Reference in Autobiography.* Princeton: Princeton University Press, 1992.

Elliott, Michael. "The Next-to-Last-Lecture: 'Wannabe Indians,' Gerald Vizenor, and *Indian Country Today*." Unpublished talk for the Modern Language Association Convention, December 28, 1994.

Ewing, Douglas. "What Is 'Stolen'? The McClain Case Revisited." In Messenger, 177–83.

Fanon, Frantz. *Black Skin, White Masks.* New York: Grove Press, 1967 [1952].

———. *The Wretched of the Earth.* New York: Grove Press, 1968 [1963].

Fernández Retamar, Roberto. "Caliban: Notes toward a Discussion of Culture in Our America." *Massachusetts Review* 15 (1974): 346–60.

Frankenberg, Ruth, and Lata Mani. "Crosscurrents, Crosstalk: Race, 'Postcoloniality,' and the Politics of Location." *Cultural Studies* (1993), 292–310.

Garcia, Mario. "Multiculturalism and American Studies." *Radical History Review* 54 (1992): 49–58.

Gates, Henry Louis, Jr. "Critical Fanonism." *Critical Inquiry* 17 (1991): 457–70.

Glancy, Diane. *Firesticks: A Collection of Stories.* Norman: University of Oklahoma Press, 1993.

Glick, Leonard B. " 'Types Distinct from Our Own': Franz Boas on Jewish Identity and Assimilation." *American Anthropologist* 84 (1982): 545–65.

Gold, Mike. *Jews without Money.* New York: Carroll and Graf, 1993 [1930].

Graulich, Melody, ed. *"Yellow Woman": Leslie Marmon Silko.* New Brunswick NJ: Rutgers University Press, 1993.

Greenblatt, Stephen. *Marvelous Possessions: The Wonder of the New World.* Chicago: University of Chicago Press, 1991.

Harris, Marvin. *Cultural Materialism: The Struggle for a Science of Culture.* New York: Vintage-Random House, 1980.

Hobsbawm, Eric, and Terence Ranger, eds. *The Invention of Tradition.* New York: Cambridge University Press, 1989.

Hochbruck, Wolfgang. " 'The Last of the Oral Tradition in Electronic Word Processing': Traditional Material and Postmodern Form in Gerald Vizenor's

Bearheart." *Proceedings of the Annual Conference for the Study of New Literatures in English*, 89–100. Essen: Die Blaue Eule Verlag, 1994.

Hogan, Linda. "The Two Lives." In *I Tell You Now: Autobiographical Essays by Native American Writers*, ed. Brian Swann and Arnold Krupat, 231–50. Lincoln: University of Nebraska Press, 1987.

Hollinger, David A. "Ethnic Diversity, Cosmopolitanism, and the Emergence of the American Liberal Intelligentsia." In *In the American Province*, ed. David A. Hollinger, 56–73. Bloomington: Indiana University Press, 1985.

Hu-Dehart, Evelyn. "Preface: The State of Native North America." In Jaimes, *Native America*, ix–x.

Hulme, Peter. *Colonial Encounters: Europe and the Native Caribbean, 1492–1797.* London: Routledge, 1992 [1986].

Hutcheon, Linda. *A Poetics of Postmodernism: History, Theory, Fiction.* New York: Routledge, 1988.

———. *The Politics of Postmodernism.* New York: Routledge, 1989.

Jaimes, M. Annette. "The Disharmonic Convergence: Leslie Silko's *Almanac of the Dead*: Review." *Wicazo Sa Review* 8 (1992): 56–57.

———, ed. *The State of Native America: Genocide, Colonization, and Resistance.* Boston: South End Press, 1992.

James, C. L. R. *The C. L. R. James Reader.* Ed. Anna Grimshaw. Oxford UK: Blackwell, 1992.

Jameson, Fredric. *The Ideologies of Theory: Essays, 1971–1986.* Vol. 2, *Syntax and History.* Minneapolis: University of Minnesota Press, 1988.

———. *Postmodernism; or, The Cultural Logic of Late Capitalism.* Durham: Duke University Press, 1991.

Jennings, Francis. *The Invasion of America: Indians, Colonialism, and the Cant of Conquest.* New York: Norton, 1975.

Judt, Tony. "The New Old Nationalism." *New York Review of Books* 41 (May 26, 1994): 44–51.

Kaplan, Alice. *French Lessons: A Memoir.* Chicago: University of Chicago Press, 1993.

Katz, Jane, ed. *This Song Remembers: Portraits of Native Americans in the Arts.* Boston: Houghton Mifflin, 1980.

King, Jaime Litvak. "Cultural Property and National Sovereignty." In Messenger, 199–208.

Krupat, Arnold. "American Histories, Native American Stories." *Early American Literature* 30 (1995): 165–74.

———. "Cosmopolitanism and Nationalism in the Criticism of Native American Literature." In *Critical Essays on Native American Literature*, ed. Alan Velie and Gerald Vizenor. Norman: University of Oklahoma Press, forthcoming.

———. *Ethnocriticism: Ethnography, History, Literature.* Berkeley: University of California Press, 1992.

———. "Native American Autobiography and the Synecdochic Self." In *American Autobiography: Retrospect and Prospect*, ed. Paul John Eakin. Madison: University of Wisconsin Press, 1991.

———. "On the Translation of Native American Literature: A Theorized History." In *On the Translation of Native American Literatures*. ed. Brian Swann. Washington DC: Smithsonian Institution Press, 1992.

———. *The Voice in the Margin: Native American Literature and the Canon*. Berkeley: University of California Press, 1989.

———. ed. *New Voices in Native American Literary Criticism*. Washington DC: Smithsonian Institution Press, 1993.

Laga, Barry. "Gerald Vizenor and His *Heirs of Columbus*: A Postmodern Quest for Discourse." *American Indian Quarterly* 18 (1994): 71–86.

Lejeune, Phillippe. "The Autobiographical Pact." *Phillippe Lejeune on Autobiography*, 3–30.

———. "The Autobiographical Pact (bis)." *Phillippe Lejeune on Autobiography*, 119–40.

———. "Autobiography in the Third Person." *Phillippe Lejeune on Autobiography*, 31–52.

———. *Phillippe Lejeune on Autobiography*. Ed. Paul John Eakin. University of Minnesota Press, 1989.

Littlefield, Daniel F., Jr. "American Indians, American Scholars, and the American Literary Canon." *American Studies* 33 (1992): 95–111.

Maffi, Mario. *The Lower East Side: Gateway to America*. New York: New York University Press, 1995.

Marks, Elaine. "Presidential Address 1993: Multiplicity and Mortality." *PMLA* 109 (1994): 366–74.

Mattina, Anthony, ed. *The Golden Woman: The Colville Narrative of Peter J. Seymour*. Trans. Anthony Mattina and Madeline de Sautel. Tucson: University of Arizona Press, 1985.

McHale, Brian. "Postmodernism; or, The Anxiety of Master Narratives," *Diacritics* 22 (1992): 17–33.

Memmi, Albert. *The Colonizer and the Colonized*. Boston: Beacon, 1965 [1957].

———. *The Pillar of Salt*. Boston: Beacon, 1992 [1955].

Messenger, Phyllis M. *The Ethics of Collecting Cultural Property: Whose Culture? Whose Property?* Albuquerque: University of New Mexico Press, 1993.

Meyer, Karl. *The Plundered Past*. New York: Atheneum, 1973.

Miller, Dallas. "Mythic Rage and Laughter: An Interview with Gerald Vizenor." *Studies in American Indian Literatures* 7 (1995): 77–96.

Mohanty, Satya K. "Epilogue: Colonial Legacies, Multicultural Futures: Relativism, Objectivity, and the Challenge of Otherness." *PMLA* 110 (1995): 108–18.

Momaday, N. Scott. *The Ancient Child*. New York: HarperCollins, 1989.

———. *House Made of Dawn*. New York: Harper-Signet, 1969 [1968].

———. *The Way to Rainy Mountain*. New York: Ballantine, 1974 [1969].

Murray, David. *Forked Tongues: Speech, Writing, and Representation in North American Indian Texts*. Bloomington: Indian University Press, 1990.

Ngũgĩ wa Thiong'o. *Decolonizing the Mind: The Politics of Language in African Literature*. London: Heinemann, 1986.

Ortiz, Simon. *Woven Stone*. Tucson: University of Arizona Press, 1992.

Owens, Louis. *Bone Game*. Norman: University of Oklahoma Press, 1994.

———. *Other Destinies: Understanding the American Indian Novel*. Norman: University of Oklahoma Press, 1992.

————. *The Sharpest Sight*. Norman: University of Oklahoma Press, 1992.

Paquin, Ron. *Not First in Nobody's Heart: The Life Story of a Contemporary Chippewa*. Ames: Iowa State University Press, 1992.

Pearce, Roy Harvey. *Savagism and Civilization: A Study of the Indian and the American Mind*. Berkeley: University of California Press, 1988 [1953].

Penn, W. S. *The Absence of Angels*. Sag Harbor NY: Permanent Press, 1994.

Pratt, Mary-Louise. *Imperial Eyes: Travel Writing and Transculturation*. London: Routledge, 1992.

Revard, Carter. "Report to the Nation: Claiming Europe." In *Earth Power Coming*, ed. Simon J. Ortiz, 166–81. Tsaile AZ: Navajo Community College Press, 1983.

Robinson, Harry. *Nature Power: In the Spirit of an Okanagan Storyteller*. Ed. Wendy Wickwire. Vancouver: Douglas and McIntyre, 1992.

————. *Write It on Your Heart*. Ed. Wendy Wickwire. Vancouver, Talon/Theytus, 1989.

Rose, Wendy. "The Great Pretenders: Further Reflections on Whiteshamanism." In Jaimes, *Native America*, 403–22.

Ruoff, A. LaVonne Brown. *American Indian Literatures: An Introduction, Bibliographic Review, and Selected Bibliography*. New York: Modern Language Association, 1990.

————. "Woodland Word Warrior: An Introduction to the Works of Gerald Vizenor." MELUS 13 (1986): 13–43.

Said, Edward. *After the Last Sky: Palestinian Lives*. New York: Pantheon, 1986.

————. *Culture and Imperialism*. New York: Knopf, 1993.

————. "Identity, Negation, and Violence." *New Left Review* 171 (1988): 226–47.

————. *The World, the Text, and the Critic*. Cambridge: Harvard University Press, 1983.

Sarris, Greg. *Keeping Slug Woman Alive: A Holistic Approach to American Indian Texts*. Berkeley: University of California Press, 1993.

Sartre, Jean-Paul. *What Is Literature?* Trans. Bernard Frechtman. New York: Philosophical Library, 1949.

Sassoon, David. "Considering the Perspective of the Victim: The Antiquities of Nepal." In Messenger, 61–72.

Scarberry-Garcia, Susan. *Landmarks of Healing: A Study of "House Made of Dawn."* Albuquerque: University of New Mexico Press, 1985.

Schubnell, Matthias. *N. Scott Momaday: The Cultural and Literary Background*. Norman: University of Oklahoma Press, 1985.

Scott, Joan Wallach. "The Campaign against Political Correctness: What's Really at Stake?" *Radical History Review* 5 (1992): 59–79.

Shell, Marc. "Marranos (Pigs); or, From Coexistence to Toleration," *Critical Inquiry* 17 (1991): 306–35.

Shohat, Ella. "Notes on the Post-Colonial." *Social Text* 31/2 (1992): 99–113.

Silko, Leslie Marmon. *Almanac of the Dead*. New York: Penguin, 1992 [1991].

————. *Ceremony*. New York: Viking, 1977.

Silko, Leslie Marmon, and James Wright. *The Delicacy and Strength of Lace*. Ed. Anne Wright. Saint Paul MN: Graywolf Press, 1986.

Smith, Henry Nash. *Virgin Land*. Cambridge: Harvard University Press, 1950.

Sollors, Werner. *Beyond Ethnicity: Consent and Descent in American Culture.* New York: Oxford University Press, 1986.

Spivak, Gayatri C. "The Making of Americans: The Teaching of English and the Future of Culture Studies." *New Literary History* 21 (1990): 781–98.

Suhonjic, Dalila. "A Plea from a Bosnian Student." *Sarah Lawrence* (Spring/Summer 1994), 16–17.

Swann, Brian. Introduction to *On the Translation of Native American Literatures,* ed. Brian Swann, xiii–xx. Washington DC: Smithsonian Institution Press, 1992.

Thrasher, Anthony Apakark. *Skid Row . . . Eskimo.* Toronto: Griffin House, 1976.

Tomlinson, John. *Cultural Imperialism: A Critical Introduction.* Baltimore: Johns Hopkins University Press, 1991.

Trafzer, Clifford. "Grandmother, Grandfather, and the First History of the Americas." In Krupat, *New Voices,* 474–87.

Turner, Terence. "Anthropology and Multiculturalism: What Is Anthropology So That Multiculturalists Should Be Mindful of It?" *Cultural Anthropology* 8 (1993): 411–29.

Vizenor, Gerald. *Bearheart: The Heirship Chronicles.* Minneapolis: University of Minnesota Press, 1990 [originally published as *Darkness in St. Louis Bearheart,* 1978].

———. "Crows Written on the Poplars: Autocritical Autobiographies." In *I Tell You Now: Autobiographical Essays by Native American Writers,* ed. Brian Swann and Arnold Krupat, 99–110. Lincoln: University of Nebraska Press, 1987.

———. *Dead Voices.* Norman: University of Oklahoma Press, 1992.

———. "The Envoy to Haiku." *Chicago Review* 39 (1993): 55–62.

———. "Gerald Vizenor, Ojibway/Chippewa Writer." In Katz, 163–68.

———. *The Heirs of Columbus.* Hanover NH: Wesleyan University Press/University Press of New England, 1991.

———. "I Know What You Mean, Erdupps MacChurbbs." In *Growing Up in Minnesota: Ten Writers Remember Their Childhoods,* ed. Chester Anderson. Minneapolis: University of Minnesota Press, 1976.

———. *Interior Landscapes: Autobiographical Myths and Metaphors.* Minneapolis: University of Minnesota Press, 1990.

———. *Manifest Manners: Postindian Warriors of Survivance.* Hanover NH: Wesleyan University Press/University Press of New England, 1994.

———. "Native American Indian Identities: Autoinscriptions and the Cultures of Names." *Genre* 26 (1992 [1993]): 1–10.

———. *The People Named the Chippewa: Narrative Histories.* Minneapolis: University of Minnesota Press, 1984.

———. "Shadow Survivance," In Vizenor, *Manifest Manners,* 63–106.

———. *Summer in the Spring: Anishinaabe Lyric Poems and Stories.* Norman: University of Oklahoma Press, 1993.

———. "The Tragic Wisdom of Salamanders." In *Sacred Trusts,* ed. Michael Katakis. San Francisco: Mercury House, 1993.

———. *The Trickster of Liberty: Tribal Heirs to a Wild Baronage.* Minneapolis: University of Minnesota Press, 1988.

————. *Wordarrows: Indians and Whites in the New Fur Trade*. Minneapolis: University of Minnesota Press, 1978.

Warren, Karen. "A Philosophical Perspective on the Ethics and Resolution of Cultural Property Issues." In Messenger, 1–26.

White, Hayden. *Metahistory: The Historical Imagination in Nineteenth-Century Europe*. Baltimore: Johns Hopkins University Press, 1973.

Whiteley, Peter. "The End of Anthropology (at Hopi)?" *Journal of the Southwest* 35 (1993): 125–57.

Wiget, Andrew. "Review of *Narrative Chance: Postmodern Discourse on Native American Indian Literatures*." *Modern Philology* 86 (1991): 476–79.

Willard, William, and Mary Kay Downing. "American Indian Studies and Intercultural Education." *Wicazo Sa Review* 7 (1991): 1–8.

Williams, Raymond. *Problems in Materialism and Culture*. London: Verso, 1980.

Zamir, Shamoon. "Literature in a 'National Sacrifice Area': Leslie Silko's *Ceremony*." In Krupat, *New Voices*, 396–418.

Zolbrod, Paul. *Reading the Voice: Native American Oral Poetry on the Written Page*. Salt Lake City: University of Utah Press, 1995.

Index

CPSIA information can be obtained at www.ICGtesting.com
Printed in the USA
BVOW05s0428270315

393553BV00015B/60/P